THE INTERNATIONAL FONDUE COOK BOOK
contains the greatest number of Fondue recipes ever
collected anywhere!

In addition, there are Wine and Cheese Directories,
Party Instructions and a Shoppers' Guide to the proper
fuels and equipment.

The Fondue is rapidly becoming a favorite food all over
the world. It makes a simple, marvelous meal!

This fascinating, thorough book enables you to expand
your knowledge and skill in this most glamorous of the
cooking arts.

The International Fondue Cook Book
Leonard Louis Levinson

A NATIONAL GENERAL COMPANY

For Bob and Evelyn
who gave me my first fondue pot

THE INTERNATIONAL FONDUE COOK BOOK
A Bantam Book / published July 1971

Published simultaneously in the United States and Canada

Bantam Books are published by Bantam Books, Inc., a National
General company. Its trade-mark, consisting of the words "Bantam
Books" and the portrayal of a bantam, is registered in the United
States Patent Office and in other countries. Marca Registrada.
Bantam Books, Inc., 666 Fifth Avenue, New York, N.Y. 10019.

PRINTED IN THE UNITED STATES OF AMERICA

"Of all books produced since the most remote ages by human talents and industry, those only that treat of cooking are, from a moral point of view, above suspicion.

"The intention of every other piece of prose may be discussed and even mistrusted; but the purpose of a cookery book is one and unmistakable. Its object can conceivably be no other than to increase the happiness of Mankind."

Thus wrote Joseph Conrad at the beginning of the century.

But is even this beyond suspicion?

He was writing the introduction of a cook book by his wife.

Acknowledgments

"RECEIVED WITH THANKS"

The above is the cheery and polite way British shop-keepers receipt their bills. And it is the phrase I wish to use in acknowledging, with gratitude, the many recipes I have been given to include in this book. There are so many people, I am going to list them alphabetically. Thank you—

Capt. Scarritt Adams, U.S.N. Ret., of Bermuda; Phil Alpert, Cheeses-of-All-Nations, N.Y.C.; Teress Altschul, Los Angeles, Calif.; Armando Armanni, Hotel Excelsior, Rome.

Rainer F. Baldauf, Señor Pico Restaurant, San Francisco, Calif.; Pierre Barrelet, Gritti Palace Hotel, Venice; Walter Baxter, The Chanterelle, London; Fred and Neill Beck, Westlake Village, Calif.; Peter S. Bugoni and staff, Baroque Restaurant, N.Y.C.

Comm. Giorgio Campione, director general of the C.I.G.A. hotels of Italy; Rosemary Cartwright of Washington, D.C.; Constance Carr of Bangor, Maine; Bruno Carvaggi of Quo Vadis Restaurant, N.Y.C.; Mr. Chacham, Cheese Unlimited, N.Y.C.; H. R. Cornwell, English Country Cheese Council, London; John Philips Cranwell, Washington, D.C.

Bruno M. Dedual, The Peninsula Hotel, Hong Kong; Marina Deserti, Bologna, Italy.

Konrad Egli, Chalet Suisse, N.Y.C.; Felice Earley, N.Y.C.

Anita Fiel, American Spice Trade Assn., N.Y.C.; Julian Freirich Co., Long Island City, N.Y.

Mrs. Doris Gospe, Santa Rosa, Calif.; Vivian Gronback, Heublein, Inc., Hartford, Conn.

John Milton Hagen, Mill Valley, Calif.; Marcia Hale, Zurich, Switzerland; Johnny Hines and Bill Smart, East Boston, Mass.; J. D'Hoir, Hotel Meurice, Paris; E. Roxie

Howlett, Diamond Walnut Kitchen, San Francisco, Calif.; Cathi Hunt, The Underwood Kitchens, Boston, Mass.; Marjorie Child Husted, Minneapolis, Minn.

Gordon Irving, Glasgow, Scotland; Herb Isaacson, Cheese Village, Ltd. and La Fondue, N.Y.C.

Paul Jacob, The Monk's Inn, N.Y.C.; Vernon Jarratt, George's Restaurant, Rome; Daryl Jason, N.Y.C.; Julius, Maître d'Hôtel, Luchow's Restaurant, N.Y.C.

Grace Teed Kent, Longchamps Restaurants, N.Y.C.; Mimi Kilgore, Tiburon, Calif.; Joe Ann Kilian, Palos Verde Peninsula, Calif.; Olga V. Kollar of Sorella Fontana, Rome and Bologna.

Rene Lasserre, Lasserre Restaurant, Paris; Mary Lehrbaummer, Oster, Milwaukee, Wisconsin; Claude Lemercier, Hotel de Crillon, Paris; Traudi Lessing, Vienna; Joyce Levinson, West Los Angeles, Calif.; Robert M. Levinson, La Cañada, Calif.; Sidnee Livingston, N.Y.C.; Paola Lucentini, N.Y.C.

Loys C. Malmgren, General Foods Kitchens, White Plains, N.Y.; Hester Marsden-Smedley, London; Matsushita Electric Corp. of America, N.Y.C.; Arnaldo Meo, Danieli Royal Excelsior Hotel, Venice; M. Miconi, Excelsior Grand Hotel Principi di Piemonte, Torino; Faith and MacGowan Miller, N.Y.C.; Gloria Mohr, San Jose, Calif.; John R. Moot, Cornwall Corp., Boston; Charles Morgenstern, Freeport, L.I., N.Y.; LaMar Mulliner, N.Y.C.; Mary Murphy, Borden, Inc., N.Y.C.

National Presto Industries, Inc., Eau Claire, Wisc.

Shirley O'Neill, Hunt-Wesson Kitchens, Fullerton, Calif.

Miss Gene Poll, The Sterno Co., N.Y.C.

Maurice Renault, Agent Littéraire, Paris; Massimo Rosati, Hotel Excelsior, Naples; Florence Rypinski, Honolulu, Hawaii.

Mimi (Mrs. Tony) Sandler, Ogilvie, Minn.; V. Schachner, Palace Hotel, Milan; Lucille Schulberg, N.Y.C.; Alice Scully, Palm Springs, Calif.; Evalyn Santiago, Solana Beach, Calif.; Bernard Simon, N.Y.C.; Maryellen Spencer, Dudley-Anderson-Yutzy, N.Y.C.; Alice Stanley, Santa Monica, Calif.; Muriel Stevens, Channel Five, Las Vegas, Nev.

Ch. Teichmann, Fouquet's Restaurant, Paris; Roger Topolinski, Restaurant Lapérouse, Paris.

Joy and Jo Van Ronkel, Beverly Hills, Calif.; Jacques Valentin, Deauville, France.

Reah Wachsman of West Los Angeles, Calif.; Charlotte Westberg, Lausanne, Switzerland; Mary Lee Gray Westcoat, Uniontown, Pa.; Arthur S. Wenzel, La Fonda Restaurant, Los Angeles, Calif., and last, but far from least, Sonia Wolfson, Beverly Hills, Calif.

Once more, I thank you from the bottom of my page.

THE AUTHOR

Contents

Introduction

The Fondue, once exclusively a Swiss dish, is rapidly becoming a favorite food-form all over the world. Especially is this true in the United States, where the humble peasant dish, served in peasant fashion, has been adopted by every layer of society as an instant party-pepper-upper, a jovial "audience-participation" meal and a delicious excuse for merry eating and drinking.

And not only in homes. In New York City there are restaurants that serve almost nothing but fondues, such as Cheeses-of-All-Nations near Wall Street, La Fondue, The Chalet Suisse, The Fondue Pot in the Swiss Center in midtown Manhattan, and The Monk's Inn, by Lincoln Center. Aspen, Colorado, boasts of The Tower Fondue Restaurant and fondues are featured at The Blue Fox and The Red Knight in San Francisco—and I am sure I am neglecting scores more.

At The Chanterelle in London they serve a Mussel Fondue; in Mousehole, Cornwall, ask Major Kelly at The Lobster Pot for his Lobster Fondue; they come from all over Paris to The Street of the Four Winds to eat both Beef and Cheese Fondues at Le Savoyard. I cannot begin to list the places in Switzerland. The Fonduta with white truffles is a specialty of the Grand Hotel Principi di Piemonte in Turin, as well as the Excelsior hotels in Rome, Naples and Florence, the Palace in Milan and the celebrated Danieli in Venice.

In Spain, Fondue Bourguignon is known as El Gran Frou Frou, in Mexico they dip tortillas in hot chili-flavored fondue. The Germans dunk a variety of wursts in their fondue, while the Dutch soak Holland rusks in theirs. The Welsh are pulling fondues out of their Rabbits and Cole Porter tells us that in Latvia, the Letts do it. The Chinese cook a great variety of meat or seafood

in a broth fondue, or Hot Pot—and finish their meal by
drinking the rich soup that remains. Hawaiian hostesses
serve fresh pineapple and papaya chunks and macadamia
nuts to dip in chocolate fondue, in Australia they use the
excellent lamb, but I have been informed, regretfully,
that there are no fondues in Samoa.

French cookbook authors are trying to make high
cuisine out of this lowly dish. The sturdy Andean moun-
taineers of Bolivia munch on their own version—as they
have been doing for centuries. And in Japan they are
making and exporting fondue sets like mad by day and
having their Teriyaki and Sukiyaki by night as usual.

Have I made my point that fondues are *international?*
And this book is just as *complete.*

For here you will find the greatest number of fondue
recipes ever collected, gathered from restaurants, institu-
tions, hotels, cooking experts and excellent home cooks
from all over—plus a number of new fondues, fresh versions and variations which I have created so that you can
amaze (and, I hope, delight) your family and friends.

It is also complete in every other phase of fondues.
There is a Directory of Cheeses suitable for fondue-ing;
party instructions; descriptions of fuels and equipment
of every nature.

We have, in this country, our choice of possibly 50
different brands of fondue paraphernalia. But actually,
you do not need any special equipment. Every kitchen
has a source of heat and a pot with which you can make
a very satisfactory fondue. The ingredients are few and
the method is simple. And if you are unfortunate enough
to be allergic to cheese, there are Beef, Seafood, Lamb,
Ham, Chicken, Fish, Hors d'Oeuvre, Vegetable and a
treasury of Dessert fondues of every flavor. As well as
Melted Vegetable, Baked and Poached Chicken, called
fondues by the French. For *fondue* is the past participle
of the French verb *fondre,* meaning "to melt," which is
where our word foundry came from.

Why all this fuss about one small subdivision of the
subject of nutrition? Well, I won't say that eating is the
most important part of our lives, but we spend about 3
hours of the 24 at table. And another 3 simply thinking
about either the last or the next meal. Then, it takes us

8 hours, more or less, to earn the money so we can eat the way we do. That comes to 14 hours, leaving 2 to digest what we've eaten and 8 hours to sleep—and dream of food.

But the fondues are more than food. They signal a social event where new friends get acquainted quickly and old ones are reunited. It is an event that is warm, cozy, intimate and appetite-stimulating. It has mystique and ritual and is at the same time simplicity itself. And it has all the conflicting legends that led to the definition of history as "a lie agreed upon."

HISTORY OF THE FONDUE

In early Greece, on the island of Samos, they made a dish which some believe to be an early cheese cake: "Take some cheese and pound it, put in a brazen sieve and strain; then add honey and flour made from spring wheat and heat the whole into one mass." However, I like to believe this was an early cheese-dessert fondue.

The Romans had something of this sort, too, and probably what Nero was fiddling with was the fire under a fondue pot of the time.

And throughout history, since the first artificer of the Iron Age invented the pot, people who had but one used it for the communal cook-and-eat-out-of meal we still retain today in the form of fondue.

Fondue legends bloom in Switzerland like the eidelweiss. A lone sheepherder, bored with his monotonous diet of bread and cheese, dropped the latter into his shepherd's pot and melted it, dipping in his bread. Then, since the fire took so long to melt the cheese, he added a belt of the local wine to hasten the process.

Another: two warring Swiss tribes, if you can imagine that, fell exhausted and hungry. One tribe had some bread, the other only cheese. They parleyed and exchanged food and, presumably, recipes. It's been "Peace, Brother!" ever since in Switzerland.

A third: Some Cinderella of the hearth dropped a piece of cheese near the fire, it melted, she ate it, and lo! she needed no fairy prince.

In any case, the cheese fondue became the national dish of Switzerland, especially popular in winter, when the nights were cold, the cheese hard and the bread stale. By adding white wine to the proportion of ⅔ of the amount of cheese, which is dredged in flour, plus a shot of kirschwasser (cherry brandy) known familiarly as kirsch, plus black pepper and nutmeg, they have come up with something almost as beautiful to the taste as the Swiss scenery is to the eye.

And, of course, the fondue became a social event after skiing and other winter sports. Along with a beef version, Fondue Bourguignon.

Legend has it that this was created in Burgundy, near the Swiss border, by a grape picker during the height of the harvest, when the pickers work feverishly to pluck the grape at the precisely right moment. Hankering for a hot meal in the middle of the day when he couldn't leave his demanding chore, he brought with him a kettle and some chunks of beef and, with the aid of oil and a fire, sizzled himself some steak between pickings. Other harvest hands joined him by dunking their beef brought from home in his hot pot and the custom spread out of the vineyard, into the home and, subsequently, all over the world.

I cannot give you actual proof that this is the way it happened. On the other hand, who is there who can rise up and say it is not so?

You would think that Chocolate Fondue would have originated in Switzerland, the home of some of the most delicious chocolate, too. But as far as I can trace the matter, it is an American creation of not too many years back.

Seafood Fondues, adaptations of age-old Oriental dishes, were first introduced here about 15 years ago by Konrad Egli, the urbane owner of Chalet Suisse in New York City.

PURCHASING FONDUE EQUIPMENT

Before buying, make sure you have the room to store your purchase. Get the recommendations of friends and relatives who have had experience with brands they can either suggest or warn you about.

Make sure the salesman demonstrates the appliance to your satisfaction. Get all the available literature and keep any instruction or recipe pamphlets that come with your equipment, especially the books from the makers of electric and butane fondue pots.

And make sure, if it is electric, that you have the proper current and voltage for the appliance in your kitchen and that it has the approval of the Underwriter's Laboratory.

It is also advisable to check that the capacity of the appliance is right for your family, your kitchen and your entertaining plans.

A section on Fondue Equipment and where to buy it appears at the end of the book.

BEFORE YOU INVITE GUESTS

Unless you have had prior experience with fondue cooking, you might try out your table-top cookery on your family first.

Remember, to have a Fondue "spectacular," be sure you have all your backstage preparations made in advance and have every "prop" or ingredient needed for the final performance right at hand when you begin your act.

Note: Don't depend on candlepower for any heat except the lowest maintenance, such as with chocolate and other dessert dips.

Make sure you have enough "gas" or fuel before you start out and have a spare tank at hand. And keep the fondue flame out of drafts or direct breeze.

Bring out your snazziest utensils: your best peppermills, silverware, china, etc.

FONDUE ENTERTAINING

Fondues are among the least difficult dishes to prepare. Aside from keeping an eagle eye and a constant stir during the creation of the cheese fondues, the rest is as easy as falling off Totie Fields.

So much is left up to the guest that he alone is responsible if his Beef Fondue meat is not done to the turn he likes best . . . or if his cube of bread falls into the cheese . . . or his piece of cake gets lost in the chocolate.

On the other hand, what your fondue diner is required to do makes him so much a part of the cooking bit that he feels he is really accomplishing something when he dips the fork and stirs it around. He is making a contribution of which he is proud, he eats as much or as little as he wants and there is none of the air pollution, flying insects and other drawbacks of the outdoor barbecue. I suppose some hostesses might not think it amiss to provide chef's caps.

And surely fondue aprons which are coming into vogue are more than decorative. They provide often-needed protection for the clothes. I was given a beautiful pink linen one, with a coquelin embroidered in gold and "Le Savoyard" in red, the last time I visited the restaurant of the same name in Paris.

And at Gimbel's in New York, recently, I purchased a small one with the word "Fondue" and an amusing little cartoon on it, price $2.50. Also, I suppose the ample cotton bar apron in the Italian national colors I received from Liguore Galliana would do nicely at a fondue party. Aprons are easy to make and any woman clever with the needle (or the sewing machine) can turn out an amusing set for her guests.

THE TABLE

Which reminds me that the table linen for a fondue party should be washable or expendable—or skipped altogether if your table is of handsome wood that defies spillage. However, even so, provide a tray under your heat source and fondue pot. In other words, be prepared for some dribble and splatter. The surface should be such that no one will have to be careful or concerned if dripping occurs. Keep everything informal.

The fondue pot goes in the center of the table, so

everyone can reach it conveniently. Have I said that 4 is the ideal number of people around 1 pot? Each place setting can have a plate with individual servings . . . or there can be a community breadbasket for the cheese fondue, one heaping platter of beef cubes for the Bourguignon, etc.

Also, in the matter of sauces, if you have enough small dishes each person can have his plate surrounded by a group of different condiments—or there can be larger bowls which are passed around, or reached over to and dipped into.

As for silverware, anything goes—and there is no hard and fast rule as to what side it goes on.

All this informality, this do-it-yourself procedure cannot help but make a fondue party light-hearted and fun-filled. Eating should always be a pleasure and this audience-participation meal should have everyone chattering and chuckling while chomping—if for no other reason than that the food of fondue is delicious and satisfying, be it mouth-watering chunks of crisp French bread soaked in lovely cheese and wine, or cubes of tender steak done to *your* turn and dunked in zesty sauces or—everyone his own candy-maker—a fat marshmallow dipped in hot chocolate or gooey butterscotch —or a party with overworked fondue pots, featuring two, three or more fondue courses! You can do it, too, for this book provides recipes from Nuts (in the Hors d'Oeuvre chapter) to Soup (in the Broth Fondues chapter).

"FONDUE" IS A WORD OF MANY MEANINGS

Recently I have detected a surge on the part of certain so-called food experts in France to transform the relatively simple Swiss dish called "fondue" into something complex and bewildering to the average cook.

Since it is difficult to tamper with the method of making it, because off-beat suggestions would prove disastrous, most of the effort to develop a mystique is concentrated around the selection of the cheeses.

Not satisfied with naming a type of cheese and its

country of origin, some French writers are concerned—in print, at least—with whether the cheeses are young or old, fat or lean, from whole milk, skim milk, or cream.

We know that different cheeses are made from the milk of the cow, the goat, the ewe—and even the water buffalo. But must we be concerned about the size of the wheel of cheese, the side of the animal the milker was positioned—or the source of the hay?

Some self-anointed Gallic experts are taking the joy out of fondue-ing by sending down papal bulls regarding protein content, percentage of salt, proportion of butter-fat and of moisture a cheese may contain before the proper *fromage* is selected for the fondue.

It is true that these days many people are educated beyond their intelligence, but it seems a pity that a fun thing like fondue may be solemnly elevated to a serious art—and "experted" to death.

My advice is to disregard the "gourmet authorities," settle for the best ingredients that are handily available and enjoy yourself at fondue-ing, no matter what the meaning of the word "fondue."

And here is a list of the principal ones.

In Switzerland it is a cheese-cum-wine-cum-seasonings dish in which crusty bread is dunked.

Also as Beef or Burgundy Fondue it is steak sizzled in very hot oil.

In France it has another meaning and my Deauville friend, Jacques Valentin, elucidated: "Since 'fondue' means 'melted' we call by that name a preparation of vegetables which, after cooking a long time in butter, fat, or oil, is completely melted. They are used as complementary elements in the preparation of many dishes." (See Melting Vegetable Fondue section.)

In the U.S. and Great Britain for many years past a fondue was a baked dish usually with bread and milk but always with cheese which melted in the oven.

Back in France a Chicken Fondue means a poached pullet. And a fondue could be a cheese filling for tarts, turnovers, croquettes or crêpes.

In the Orient especially a fondue is similar to a Burgundy Fondue—except that instead of hot oil, hot broth is the cooking agent. Shellfish, other meats in addition to beef, and vegetables are also cooked. And at the end of the meal, the broth is sipped as soup.

Newest type of fondue is the American Seafood and Fish Fondues, using court bouillon, condensed soup or consommé as the hot liquid in which the food is cooked.

Dessert fondues are also quite new. Not only various kinds of chocolate, but butterscotch, cream and other delicious hot coatings are used with almost anything sweet as the dunking material.

Since I wrote *The Complete Book of Low-Calorie Cooking,* I've been asked if I could provide a low-calorie fondue.

Cheese, wine, milk, etc., are high in caloric content— and so is beef and oil—so there is nothing I could recommend . . . except you can slightly reduce the calories in chocolate fondues by using bittersweet chocolate bars or squares or Droste or Van Houten powdered plain chocolate, plus a non-caloric sweetener in place of sugar.

Around the World
in 18 Fondue Pots

One of the loveliest of women and one of the most heart-stopping ballerinas of the age is the peerless Tamara Toumanova—and I've been a fan ever since she came here with the De Basil Ballet Russe. So, when she learned of this fondue book, wouldn't you know she would contribute probably the most glamorous fondue we have?

FONDUE A LA TOUMANOVA
[Serves 4]

1 cup dry vermouth
2 tablespoons butter
½ pound (2 cups) cubed mild Cheddar cheese
3 tablespoons flour
1 3-ounce package cream cheese, at room temperature
½ cup Benedictine
1 teaspoon sugar
¼ teaspoon nutmeg
¼ teaspoon cayenne
Salt to taste

Pour vermouth into fondue pot over low heat. When it is hot, add butter. When butter has melted, add cheese cubes that have been dredged in the flour. Stir constantly until cheese is completely melted. Add cream cheese and stir until well blended with the rest of the mixture. Stir into this the Benedictine, sugar, nutmeg, cayenne and salt. Yumm!

From Jacques Valentin of Deauville:

FONDUE FRIBOURGEOISE

Prepared in a pipkin or earthenware pot or casserole with handle.

Place thinly sliced Vacherin cheese and some white Fendant wine in pot, which has been rubbed with clove of garlic first. Heat and stir melting cheese with wooden spoon to get a smooth creamy consistency. At finish, flavor with ground pepper and a bit of nutmeg.

Drink snifters of Fendant wine to wash down the fondue-soaked bread.

Fondue Neuchâteloise is made the same way, except fresh or aged Gruyère cheese is used (see Index).

FONDUE AU FROMAGE (French Cheese Fondue)
[Serves 4 to 6]

3 cups (¾ pound) diced Comté, Beaufort, or Gruyère cheese (or all 3 mixed)	Salt and white pepper Powdered nutmeg
2 tablespoons flour	1½ tablespoons butter
1 clove garlic, peeled	¼ cup heavy cream
1¾ cups Chablis	3 tablespoons cherry liqueur
	1½ loaves long, thin French bread

Dredge cheese in flour or shake together in bag.

In top of double boiler over direct heat, boil garlic and wine until liquid is reduced to ¾ths. Strain and remove garlic and return wine to pot, this time over boiling water. Add cheese, a handful at a time, stirring until each is melted before adding next. Add salt, pepper and nutmeg to taste, and blend. Add butter and 2 tablespoons of the cream and mix well. As fondue thickens, add rest of cream gradually, then stir in the liqueur.

Transfer to fondue pot over low heat at table. Serve with the French bread, cut into 1-inch squares, with crust on at least 1 side.

Dunk and stir. If fondue gets too thick, thin with some Chablis, warmed, or warm cream.

This fondue came to me from a friend who lives in Chelsea, the Latin Quarter of London.

FLAMING FONDUE
[Serves 8]

1 quart and 3 ounces dry white wine
2¼ pounds Gruyère cheese, in very thin slices
3 tablespoons flour
½ cup kirsch

This special occasion dish should be made in a copper pan, if possible, but in any case one with a very thick bottom.

Put 1 quart of wine in pan and heat. Stir in cheese slices and cook gently until melted.

With the 3 ounces of wine, blend the flour into a smooth paste. Stir some of the wine-cheese mixture into the paste and transfer all back into pan and keep stirring until mixture thickens.

Pour into a dish; add the kirsch and set liqueur alight just as you bring dish to table. Eaten by dipping in squares of French bread at the end of wooden forks.

NORWEGIAN MEAT BALL FONDUE
[Makes about 30]

⅓ cup breadcrumbs
⅔ cup milk
1 pound very lean ground beef
1 teaspoon instant minced onion or 1 tablespoon
minced onion
2 teaspoons minced parsley
Salt and pepper to taste
1 tablespoon flour
Peanut oil
1 teaspoon salt

All ingredients should be at room temperature.

Simmer breadcrumbs in milk, remove, press dry, mix with beef, onion, parsley and salt and pepper. Add enough of the milk to bind beef when made into walnut-sized balls. Roll in the flour or shake balls and flour together in paper bag.

Heat oil in fondue pot to 370° and add teaspoon salt. Using wooden skewers or fondue forks, each diner cooks his own meat balls in hot oil until done, from 1 to 1½ minutes.

Serve with cranberry-like lingonberries, or whole cranberry sauce, dill or vinaigrette sauces.

Variation: Surprise Meat Ball Fondue: Proceed as above, but when meat mixture is blended, have sufficient Jarlsberg or Gruyère cheese, cut in ¼-inch cubes, and press meat around each cube so cheese is completely covered. Then continue dredging balls in flour and cooking as before.

Paul Jacob, owner of The Monk's Inn, a picturesque restaurant on the upper west side of New York City, contributed the Norwegian Meat Ball recipe, as well as the one that follows, which comes from Bolivia.

QUESU MACHA
[Serves 4]

1 pound goat cheese (if Bolivian Queso de Cabra is unobtainable, use Monterey Jack, Goat Cheese from Lorraine, Chevrotin, La Mothe, Chevre de la Brie, or the Italian Formaggio di Capra), grated

Flour

Olive oil

Cayenne or paprika

Form cheese into smallish balls and bind with flour. Coat with more flour.

Heat oil to just below smoking and cook skewered cheese balls until golden crust is formed. Remove, dust with smidgen of cayenne or paprika and dip into sauces, such as Tartar, Mustard, Tomato, Pepper, etc.

WELSH FONDUE
[Serves 4 to 6]

1 leek, peeled

4 ounces (1 stick) butter

4 tablespoons flour

3 cups milk, warmed

4 cups (1 pound) Caerphilly cheese, cubed or coarsely shredded

1 teaspoon salt

Fresh-ground pepper

Rub inside of fondue pot and wooden stirring spoon with leek. Discard.

In pot, melt butter, add flour and blend well. Add warmed milk and stir until smooth. Add cheese and stir continually until melted and mixture is thick and creamy. Add salt and pepper to taste, blending thoroughly.

Another country heard from with a regional fondue was Germany.

BAVARIAN FONDUE
[Serves 4]

1½ cups imported German beer	1 tablespoon potato flour or cornstarch
4 cups (1 pound) Muenster cheese, in small dice	1 teaspoon salt
2 tablespoons water	¼ teaspoon fresh-cracked black pepper

Pinch nutmeg

In double boiler over boiling water, heat beer to a boil; add handful of cheese at a time, stirring each batch until it melts before adding next.

Mix potato flour and water, adding seasonings, until you have a smooth paste. Blend this into cheese-beer mixture and cook, stirring constantly, until thickened.

Transfer to fondue pot over medium heat and invite guests to begin dunking crusty bread cubes.

ITALIAN FONTINA SANDWICHES
[Serves 4]

1 cup cubed Fontina cheese	Salt, pepper, paprika
Milk to cover	5 tablespoons butter
4 eggs, beaten	4 slices French toast

Soak cheese cubes in milk to cover for 1 hour. Mix with beaten eggs, season with salt, pepper and paprika.

In saucepan, melt butter, stir in cheese-milk-egg mixture. Scramble over very low heat until mixture is creamy.

Pour over slices of French toast on individual plates and serve at once.

In addition to cooking in an earthenware fondue pot, as for Fondue Americana below, cheese fondues can also be made in chafing dishes over simmering water, or in the top of a double boiler over hot water and transferred to a fondue pot or attractive flameproof dish kept hot over some source of heat—alcohol, Sterno, electric grill or butane stove.

FONDUE AMERICANA
[Serves 4]

1½ pounds American cheese, shredded
1 teaspoon dry mustard
½ teaspoon onion salt
¼ teaspoon nutmeg
2 8-ounce cans tomato sauce with cheese
1 cup flat beer

Melt cheese in earthenware fondue pot over low flame. Stir in mustard, onion salt and nutmeg. Gradually add tomato sauce and beer, stirring all the time with wooden spoon until smooth.

Dunk bread cubes on fondue forks or skewers or dip in sticks of celery or carrot.

On the lower East Side of New York there is a traditional drink called an Egg Cream, which has neither egg nor cream, but consists of a shot of milk and a shot of chocolate syrup with soda water to fill the glass. However, this next fondue does contain both eggs and cream.

EGG-CREAM FONDUE
[Serves 4 or 5]

¼ cup butter or margarine
1½ tablespoons flour
¼ teaspoon salt
¼ teaspoon fresh-ground
pepper
1 cup cream
3 egg yolks, slightly beaten
6 tablespoons grated Parmesan cheese

Melt butter in fondue pot over low heat; add flour, stirring until frothy. Add salt, pepper and the cream all at once. Cook, stirring constantly, until mixture thickens.

Pour a dollop of the sauce into the egg yolks, stirring constantly, then pour this into pot of sauce, stirring over low heat until thickened, about 2 minutes. Add cheese and stir well until blended. If too thick, add 1 to 2 tablespoons more cream, but no more. Fondue should be thick enough to coat dippers without dripping.

Dippers: Green and sweet red pepper strips, carrot bites, celery strips, squares of apple, the usual French bread cubes, yellow and red tiny tomatoes.

CALIFORNIA FONDUE
[Serves 4 to 6]

1 cut clove garlic	3 tablespoons flour
2 cups dry white California wine	½ teaspoon salt
	½ teaspoon paprika
1 pound Monterey Jack cheese, in small cubes	3 tablespoons California brandy

Use halved clove of garlic to rub wooden stirring spoon and fondue pot.

Heat wine in pot until small bubbles appear.

Meanwhile shake cheese in bag with flour, coating well. Slowly add cheese by small handfuls to wine, stirring until mixture bubbles. Add salt and paprika, then brandy, mixing well. Dunk with chunks of sourdough bread, each piece having at least one crust side.

MEXICAN FONDUE
[For 4 to 6]

¼ cup olive oil	4 drops Tabasco sauce
1 clove garlic, minced	2 teaspoons flour
1 large onion, fine-chopped	1 tablespoon butter
3 sweet red peppers	1 cup heavy cream
1½ cups shredded sharp Cheddar cheese	Tortillas, French bread or English muffins,
Salt and fresh-ground pepper	toasted and cut in 1-inch squares

Heat oil in skillet, fry garlic and onion.

Roast peppers over flame and peel; remove stem and seeds; cut into pieces.

Put oil, garlic, onion and peppers in blender and purée.

Put into cheese fondue pot and heat with cheese, stirring until it is melted; add seasonings.

Knead flour into butter and add, little by little, to simmering sauce. Stir until smooth. Add cream and continue stirring until bubbling.

Using wooden forks, dunk toasted bread or muffin squares in pot.

AUSTRALIAN LAMB FONDUE
[Serves 4]

1½ pounds cubed tender leg of lamb, trimmed of all fat	Cooking oil (peanut, coconut, sunflower seed, safflower seed, olive, cooking, salad, etc.)

Proceed as with Beef Fondue (see Index).

Serve with Mint (see below), Hot Curry, Horseradish and/or Garlic Sauces.

Variation: For ½ pound of the lamb, substitute 2 lamb kidneys, cored and all fat cut away, and cubed.

MINT SAUCE FOR LAMB FONDUE
[Makes 1 cup]

12 sprigs fresh mint	2 teaspoons salt
4 tablespoons vinegar	½ teaspoon fresh-ground pepper
3 tablespoons minced onion	
1 cup salad oil	½ teaspoon paprika

Wash mint and chop leaves fine. Mix remaining ingredients together; add mint and blend well.

This is a recipe for the electric Panasonic Party Cooker, which is like a metal fondue pot with a wide lip for draining. Recipe can be made in regular alcohol or Sterno-heated pot by regulating heat manually.

EAST-WEST TEMPURA
[Serves 4]

1 pound raw shrimp, shelled and deveined	1 green pepper, seeded and sliced
½ pound flounder, sole or other firm white fish, in 1-inch cubes	1 raw sweet potato, pared, cut into sticks
½ pound scallops, halved	1 raw white potato, pared, cut into thin slices

Batter

3 eggs	1 teaspoon salt
1½ cups all-purpose flour	1 teaspoon baking powder
1½ cups water	¼ teaspoon ground ginger
2 tablespoons cornstarch	Peanut or salad oil for deep frying

Arrange prepared seafood and vegetables in eye-pleasing pattern on large, flat tray; cover with plastic or aluminum foil, wrap and chill in refrigerator until serving time.

Make batter by beating eggs, adding flour, water, cornstarch, salt, baking powder and ginger and blending well until smooth. Chill until serving time.

Set automatic thermal control of cooker to 360° and pour in salad oil to mark (approximately 4 cups). Heat until pilot light goes off. Or use deep fat thermometer.

Bring meats and vegetables and batter to table. Each guest skewers several pieces of seafood and vegetable onto bamboo skewer, dips it into batter, holds it over batter bowl to allow excess batter to drip off.

Then he cooks skewered food in hot fat until golden brown, removes and rests skewer on draining rack for several minutes.

Serve with several sauces from the list on pages 117–136 and lemon and/or lime wedges.

The venerable but sprightly Peninsula Hotel in Hong Kong has an executive staff of Swiss lineage. The cheese fondue served is traditional to Switzerland and I am indebted to Bruno M. Dedual, the food and beverage manager, for the recipe.

PENINSULA CHEESE FONDUE
[Serves 1]

7 tablespoons dry white wine
1 small clove garlic, crushed
3 ounces Gruyère cheese,
    grated (3/4 cup)
3 ounces Emmentaler cheese,
     grated (3/4 cup)
Grind of fresh-ground
    pepper
Nutmeg to taste
1 teaspoon kirsch
½ teaspoon cornstarch

Place wine, garlic and cheeses in fondue pot or casserole. Add the seasonings and bring to a boil slowly, stirring until all the cheese has melted.

Mix the kirsch and cornstarch together and add to the pot. Blend well and use as dip with cubes of crisp French bread.

FONDUE A LA RUSSE

Proceed as above, but instead of kirsch, use ¼ cup vodka.

Hors D'Oeuvre Fondues

"Men become passionately attached to women who know how to cosset them with delicate tidbits."—HONORÉ DE BALZAC

Almost every fondue in this book can be used as an appetizer, a feature at a cocktail or other party, or a midnight snack.

And, likewise, every dish in this section can be used as a regular-meal fondue.

For fondues occupy that special position on any menu —the starring dish—which is the focal point by reason of being cooked, or cooking, at the table or buffet . . . and being a help-yourself item that is so very attractive it brings the guest back to the pot, time after time.

An unusual appetizer can be made in an oil fondue pot using wild rice, which must be of the best quality and this year's crop.

POPPED WILD RICE

Do not wash rice; place in small amounts in a fine strainer, sieve or colander. Lower into oil or fat at 375° for just long enough to pop—one or two seconds. Lift out and spread on paper towels. Salt to taste. Serve at once.

Señor Pico is a delightful early Californian and Mexican restaurant in a picturesque mall in San Francisco. Rainer F. Baldauf of that establishment sent me this recipe, which means "Chili with Cheese."

CHILI CON QUESO
[Makes 4½ cups]

3 cups half-and-half
½ pound Monterey Jack
   cheese, grated
¼ pound New York Cheddar
   cheese, grated
2 tablespoons minced onion
1 small clove garlic, minced
1 tablespoon butter

6 tablespoons white wine
¼ cup cornstarch
¼ cup cold water
¼ cup chopped *jalapeño*
   chilies
Salt
Coarsely ground white
   pepper

Tostado chips

In upper half of double boiler, heat the half-and-half; add cheeses and set over low heat to melt.

In small skillet or pan sauté the onion and garlic in the butter until onion is transparent; add 3 tablespoons of the wine, swish around and pour all into cheese mixture, blending well.

Put hot water in bottom of double boiler, place top over and set over fire.

Mix cornstarch and water until well blended. Thicken cheese mixture with this combination, stirring constantly. Add chilies, salt and pepper to taste and remaining 3 tablespoons of wine; mix thoroughly.

Keep pot over hot water until ready to use. Serve in fondue pot for cocktails, with tostado chips for dipping.

And a simpler South-of-the-Border version.

CHILI FONDUE
[Serves 6]

1 15-ounce can chili con carne
1 8-ounce can tomato sauce

1 tablespoon cornstarch
4 ounces Cheddar cheese,
   shredded

In pan, heat chili until it boils.

Mix tomato sauce with cornstarch and add to chili. Bring to boil again, while stirring. Add cheese and heat until it melts and mixture thickens.

Transfer to fondue pot and keep hot. Dip in Fritos, other corn chips, crackers, or carrot and celery sticks.

I think we should have one or two cold fondues, don't you?

This one is made by beating all of the ingredients together, either with a French whip, an egg-beater or in the blender.

A COLD MEXICAN FONDUE
[Makes about 3 cups]

½ cup chili sauce
1 8-ounce package cream cheese, at room temperature
1 tablespoon lime juice

2 teaspoons chili powder
⅛ teaspoon garlic powder
Dash Tabasco sauce
1 cup sour cream
¼ cup dry sherry

Beat chili sauce, cream cheese, lime juice, chili powder, garlic powder and Tabasco together until homogenized. Beat in sour cream and sherry. Chill.

Serve with tostados, Fritos, cheese curls, potato chips, crackers, Melba toast, rye thins or shredded wheat squares.

SEAFOOD SAUCE FONDUE
[Makes 1½ cups]

½ cup mayonnaise
½ cup sour cream or yogurt
2 tablespoons chili sauce or catsup

1 tablespoon mild wet mustard
½ teaspoon prepared horse-radish (optional)

1 tablespoon lemon juice

This is a cold dip for cooked seafood (lobster, crab, scallops, shrimp, fried oysters and clams).

Combine ingredients and stir until smooth. A tablespoon of capers may be added.

SHRIMP IN BOCK BEER BATTER
[Serves 8 to 10]

2 pounds fresh raw shrimp, shelled and cleaned

Batter

1 cup sifted flour	2 eggs, beaten
1 tablespoon baking powder	2 tablespoons melted butter
2 tablespoons sugar	½ cup dark beer
¼ teaspoon salt	½ cup milk

Oil for deep frying

Ahead: Rinse, drain, devein and thoroughly dry shrimp, then butterfly by slitting almost in half and opening.

Make batter by sifting flour, baking powder, sugar and salt together. Then stir in eggs, butter, beer and milk.

At table: Dip shrimp into batter 2 at a time. Fry them in hot (375°) oil or fat in metal fondue pot until golden brown. Drain on paper towels.

Serve with Hot-Cold Seafood Cocktail Sauce (see below) or Tart Fruit Sauce which is your choice of fruit jelly to which ¼ as much Horseradish Sauce has been added, the both mixed in electric blender. They also throw in French-fried potatoes at Luchow's.

HOT-COLD SEAFOOD COCKTAIL SAUCE
[Makes over 1 cup]

¾ cup chili sauce	1 tablespoon Worcester-
2½ tablespoons ground horse-	shire sauce
radish	1 teaspoon grated onion
3 tablespoons lemon juice	½ teaspoon Tabasco sauce

Blend all ingredients thoroughly. Serve over seafood for cocktails.

SHRIMP FONDUE
[Serves 6 to 8 as appetizer]

1 clove garlic
1 can frozen condensed cream
    of shrimp soup, thawed

1 cup diced Emmentaler
    cheese
Fresh-ground pepper
2 tablespoons dry white wine

Rub fondue pot and wooden stirring spoon with garlic; discard.

Pour soup and cheese into fondue pot and heat until cheese melts, stirring continually. Season with pepper to taste; stir in wine when well heated.

Dip rye or French bread chunks into pot.

QUICKIE FONDUE

3 cups oil
1 teaspoon salt
Frozen breaded shrimp,
    thawed

Frozen breaded scallops,
    thawed
Frozen egg rolls, thawed

Heat oil and salt in fondue pot until 1-inch cube of soft bread browns in 40 to 50 seconds. This is done on kitchen range at high heat or in electric fondue pot heated at highest setting for 15 minutes.

Spear 1 egg roll, shrimp or scallop and cook about 1 minute, until golden. Guests repeat until all on platter is gone.

Sauces suggested: Sweet 'n' Sour, Hot Mustard, Soy, Tartar.

PIZZA FONDUE
[Serves 4 to 6 as main dish, 10 to 12 as appetizer]

2 tablespoons margarine or
    shortening
½ pound ground beef
1 onion, chopped
1 tablespoon cornstarch
1½ teaspoons fennel seed
1½ teaspoons oregano

¼ teaspoon garlic powder
2 10½-ounce cans pizza
    sauce
2½ cups grated Cheddar
    cheese
1 cup grated Mozzarella
    cheese

Melt shortening in skillet or fondue pot at high heat and brown meat and onion, stirring briskly. Reduce heat to medium.

Mix cornstarch, fennel, oregano and garlic powder with pizza sauce and add to meat and onions. Stir well and heat. When mixture thickens and bubbles, add cheeses a handful at a time, stirring well after each addition. Blend until smooth and melted.

Keep fondue bubbling on medium heat and serve with toasted garlic bread cubes, squares of toasted English muffin, or dunk breadsticks.

SWISS FONDUE SANDWICHES
[Serves 6]

6 eggs	Salt and pepper to taste
½ cup (1 stick) soft butter	More butter
½ cup grated Emmentaler or Gruyère cheese	6 slices fresh-made French toast

Separate the eggs and beat the whites until stiff. Add the yolks one by one, stirring after each is added. Blend in butter and cheese. Season with salt and pepper.

Cook exactly like scrambled eggs, using butter.

Divide among six warm plates with a slice of French toast on each.

This is what you might call another deep-fat appetizer which might be served on a buffet table with the hostess doing the cooking pre-dinner before the eyes of the guests.

CHEESE PUFFS
[Makes 20 puffs]

4 egg whites	1½ cups grated Parmesan cheese
½ teaspoon salt	
Sprinkle cayenne	Cooking oil
Paprika	

Beforehand, beat egg whites until stiff, season with salt and cayenne. Stir in grated Parmesan, mixing thoroughly.

Heat fat in fondue pot or chafing dish blazer pan to 360°–375° and bring to table, placing over flame or electric heat which will maintain temperature.

Drop batter by teaspoonfuls into oil and cook until delicately browned on all sides. Remove with slotted spoon and drain on paper towels. Sprinkle with paprika and serve at once.

DARYL'S FONDUE
[Serves 4 as main dish, 8 to 12 as buffet dip]

1 tablespoon butter or margarine
¾ cup coffee cream (or non-dairy substitute)
3 cups Muenster cheese, in small cubes

1 teaspoon lemon juice
1 tablespoon mayonnaise
½ teaspoon dry mustard (or to taste)
Sprinkle garlic salt

Melt butter in fondue pot, add cream and heat well; add cheese, 1 cup at a time, stirring and melting. Add lemon juice, mayonnaise, mustard and garlic salt and keep stirring until mixture is smooth.

Use as a dip with breadsticks, etc.

Variation: Using 2 cups of cheese, this makes a fine sauce for eggs, as in Eggs Benedict.

ALL-AMERICAN FONDUE
[Serves 10 as hors d'oeuvre]

3 cups Sauterne
1 tablespoon lemon juice
1 pound (4 cups) grated Colby cheese
1½ tablespoons flour

3 tablespoons applejack
⅛ teaspoon chili powder
2 loaves sourdough bread, from San Francisco if possible

In saucepan or top of double boiler heat wine over low flame until small bubbles rise around edge. Add lemon juice and stir.

Shake grated cheese in bag with flour, or dredge. Add to wine by ½-cups, stirring and melting between additions, using wooden spoon. When all cheese has been melted, add applejack and chili powder. Stir 1 minute; transfer to fondue pot over heat that will keep fondue at a slow bubble.

Meanwhile, cut bread into 1-inch cubes so that each piece has at least 1 crust. You can use day-old bread, or toast it lightly. Hand each eater a long fondue fork, to which he affixes a square of bread, which he then swirls in the fondue until it is well coated—and the mixture well stirred. Remove, drip off excess fondue over pot and transfer to mouth carefully.

TWO-CHEESE FONDUE
[Makes about 2½ cups as a dip, or serves 4]

3 tablespoons butter	1 teaspoon instant minced
3 tablespoons flour	onion
Dash cayenne	1 cup (¼ pound) Parmesan
¾ cup light cream	cheese, grated
¾ cup chicken broth	1 cup (¼ pound) Emmen-
	taler cheese, grated

Melt butter in fondue pot over good heat; blend in flour and cayenne with wooden spoon. Continue stirring while gradually adding cream and chicken broth. Add onion and cook, stirring, until thickened. Add cheeses, ½ cupful at a time, until melted, while stirring.

Place pot over medium flame on table and serve as a dip with toasted chunks of rye or pumpernickel bread. Or for 4 guests at dinner.

In Prohibition days, one of the most celebrated of sniffer-outers of liquor-law violators had the colorful name of Pussyfoot Johnson. So what could be more appropriate than to call a liquorless fondue after him?

PUSSYFOOT FONDUE
[Serves 8 to 10 as appetizer]

1 clove garlic (optional)
2 cups apple juice or cider
½ pound Gruyère cheese, in shreds (2 cups)
½ pound Emmentaler cheese, in shreds (2 cups)
1 tablespoon cornstarch
3 tablespoons lemon juice
Paprika, nutmeg, or fresh-ground pepper

Perfume interior of fondue pot by rubbing with cut clove of garlic.

Add apple juice and simmer over low heat; when bubbles begin to surface, slowly add cheeses, a handful at a time, stirring continually with wooden spoon, until all cheese is melted.

Blend cornstarch and lemon juice; stir into pot and blend well. Add either paprika, nutmeg or pepper to taste. Stir and cook until fondue is smooth and thicker. Dip in cubes of French bread.

CAULIFLOWERETS

Crisp, cold sections of cauliflower make a delicious appetizer dipper. Select a fresh head of cauliflower, trim it and soak in ice water and 1 tablespoon vinegar for 1 hour. Drain thoroughly, break into flowerets, serve on platter, either plain or sprinkled with paprika, for a cocktail dip.

SAUSAGE AND CHEESE FONDUE
[Serves 6 to 8 as appetizer]

½ pound of favorite sausage
½ pound of favorite Swiss cheese
Cooking oil
2 tablespoons butter
Slice raw potato

Skin sausage and cut into ⅔-inch cubes. Trim cheese of rind and cut into as many cubes as you have of sausage. Thread 1 sausage cube and 1 of cheese on wooden skewers.

Fill fondue pot with 2 inches of oil, plus butter, and bring to boil in kitchen. Add potato (to prevent spattering) and bring to table or buffet and keep hot over Sterno or electric plate. Bring platter of skewered sausage and cheese alongside.

Guests dip these into oil until cheese is about to melt, then remove and eat when cool enough. Skewers should be long enough so guests have no danger of burning fingers with oil. If metal forks are used, transfer cooked food to cold one before approaching the mouth.

FRANKFURTER FONDUE
[Makes 32 appetizers]

1½ cups Cheddar or American cheese, in cubes

½ cup milk
1 8-ounce can tomato sauce

8 frankfurters, each cut into 4

Melt cheese and milk in fondue pot or double boiler over hot water. Add tomato sauce, heat and stir until well blended.

Broil frankfurter chunks and stick with wooden skewers or toothpicks. Dunk in fondue pot and coat well. Remove and dip into mustard, pickle relish or Worcestershire sauce set out in small bowls.

WESTERN BEEF FONDUE
[Makes 12 appetizer servings]

1½ pounds beef tenderloin in ¾-inch cubes

Beef Fondue Sauce (see below)

Cooking oil

Pour oil into metal fondue pot or electric skillet to depth of 2 inches and heat to 400°.

Spear beef cubes on wooden fondue forks or skewers and cook until done to each guest's taste.

Dip into Beef Fondue Sauce or in condiments, as done at the Restaurant Franziskaner in Zurich. They offer:

Tartar sauce
Mustard-flavored mayonnaise
Sour cream
Béarnaise sauce

Chopped sweet or sour pickles
Chutney (chopped)
Minced pickled peaches
Minced onion and scallions

BEEF FONDUE SAUCE
[Makes more than 1 cup]

1 8-ounce can tomato sauce
1 tablespoon seasoned vinegar (wine, tarragon, etc.)
1 teaspoon sugar

1 teaspoon prepared horseradish
1 teaspoon Worcestershire
  sauce
½ clove garlic, crushed

Mix and blend all ingredients well.

Another sauce for Beef Fondues:

VERY RICH STEAK SAUCE
[Makes over 1 cup]

¼ cup olive oil
1 onion, chopped fine
4 sprigs parsley, chopped
  fine
1 cup red wine
2 tablespoons lemon juice

½ tablespoon minced tarragon
½ tablespoon sugar
2 teaspoons salt
⅛ teaspoon fresh-crushed
  pepper

4 tablespoons butter

Heat oil in skillet, add onion and parsley and cook until onion is limp. Add all other ingredients except butter; mix well and cook over low heat 5 minutes.

Stir in butter and serve hot with any Beef Fondue.

HENRY FONDUE
[Serves 4 to 6; double as hors d'oeuvre]

2 ounces (½ stick) butter
1 medium onion, minced
¼ cup flour
½ cup puréed chicken livers
½ cup tomato paste
½ cup cream

1½ tablespoons Worcester-
   shire sauce
1 teaspoon salt
¼ teaspoon Tabasco sauce
½ cup Parmesan cheese,
   grated fine

2 ounces (¼ cup) brandy

Melt butter in pan and sauté onion until tender; add flour and cook for 5 minutes, stirring constantly. Add chicken livers and cook 3 minutes more. Add tomato paste, cream, Worcestershire, salt and Tabasco and stir until smooth.

Cook an additional 15 minutes, stirring continually.

Remove from heat, add cheese and stir until melted. Blend in brandy; pour into fondue pot and keep hot. Dunk with French, rye or wholewheat bread chunks.

Cheese Fondues

"This is a dish for the young—and for people with hearty digestions."—French gourmet.

"La Fondue," wrote the late Philip Harben in his *Cookery Encyclopaedia*, "is a famous, in fact about the only famous, Swiss national dish. Indeed it is more than a dish, it is something of a social occasion, for the eating of it is as interesting and important as the cooking."

CHEESE FACTS

One pound of cheese contains the protein and fat of a gallon of whole milk.

Too high temperature and too long over heat will overcook cheese so that it is lumpy, stringy and tough.

To keep cheese smooth and tender in a milk sauce, add the grated or shredded cheese to cold milk and heat slowly.

To keep cheese, cover with wax paper, then with a piece of cheesecloth well dampened with vinegar. This will stop mold from forming. Don't keep cheese in tightly covered jars.

IF YOUR CHEESE FONDUE THICKENS

Thin it down a bit with warm white wine (if you've used wine) or milk (if it's a non-alcoholic fondue).

But M. Cochet, the *patron* of Au Savoyard in Paris recommends that you drop the yolk of an egg into thickened cheese fondue and stir briskly.

He recommends, also, that you leave the kirsch out

of the list of ingredients and instead, serve a glass to each guest, so that you can dip the bread cube into the liqueur before dipping it into the fondue pot. Different!

NOTE OF CAUTION ON THE COOKING OF CHEESE

Cheese fondues take a bit of care, since cheese in cooking is a delicate ingredient. First, you need a pan or pot with a heavy bottom, to distribute the heat evenly. And the bottom should be "blunt" or flat, for the same reason. Second, the amount of heat is important, because the consistency of the fondue depends on it not getting too hot and tough or stringy or separating or burning, and not remaining too cold. Third, stir, stir, stir—keep stirring while cooking, to blend all the elements into that smooth, creamy mixture which you achieve with the perfect fondue. Use a wooden spoon, fork or spatula, or a French wire whisk. And be alert to offer the fondue to your guests at the peak moment.

In most recipes it is recommended that the cheese be cut into small cubes before adding it to the pot, and sometimes it is to be sliced thin. These are better ways than grating or shredding, according to the consensus of cheese-masters. Be sure you use very dry Gruyère or Emmentaler in your fondue, and do not overcook, or it may come out stringy, like the same cheese in onion soup.

Unless otherwise stated, all cheese ingredients are to be at room temperature when the recipe begins.

ON STIRRING

In stirring the fondue pot to melt the cheese and in stirring the bread or other dunking material, there are no less than three schools of thought.

First there is the Clockwise or conservative school which stirs to the right. Next come the members of the Counter-clockwise group who are, naturally, looked upon as leftists. Then there is the Figure-8 advocates who swirl their mixing spoons and fondue forks in both the clock and counter directions. These are the same people who drive their cars down the middle of the road, no matter how fast or slow they go. It is wisest not to tangle your fork with them while they are figure-eighting.

TO DRINK WITH CHEESE FONDUES

In Switzerland only hot tea or white wine is drunk with cheese fondues. Latter include Fendant from shores of Lake Leman; Aizle and Yvonne from the Rhone Valley; in France they have Muscadet, Sauvignon or Sancerre, Riesling of Alsace and the wine of Arbois.

But never iced drinks.

My introduction to the whole fondue bit took place many years ago in Paris when Wolfe Kaufman took me to Le Savoyard and introduced me to M. Cochet, the *patron*. He recommended the cheese fondue from Savoie and I've been an addict ever since.

Beaufort, a cheese of Savoie, is available all year, according to André Simon, but if it is not available in your neighborhood, use Gruyère instead.

FONDUE "AU SAVOYARD"
[Serves 2]

¼ pound (1 cup) Beaufort cheese, diced	2 tablespoons kirsch
	1 clove garlic, on toothpick
½ pound (1 cup) Emmentaler cheese, diced	Pinch nutmeg
	2 egg yolks
½ cup dry white wine	More kirsch

Melt in fondue pot the cheeses, wine, kirsch, seasoned by garlic (which is removed before serving), and nutmeg. Use low flame, stirring constantly until well mixed.

After the fondue eaters and the heat have reduced fondue to half or less of original volume, add beaten egg yolks and more kirsch.

Each diner is supplied with toasted chunks of crusty French bread and a wooden fork. Bread is dipped and turned in cheese mixture, drained a bit, and eaten as soon as cool enough.

Variation: A different taste may be achieved by having the kirsch in a separate container and dip bread in that before dipping it in the fondue. This makes it more crusty.

In the Jura Mountains of eastern France, one of the leading cheeses is Comté (the region is called Franche-Comté), very similar to Gruyère, which is made across the border in Switzerland in the Gruyère Valley. Both are similar to Emmentaler (named for the next valley to Gruyère) but with much smaller holes.

Defective wheels of Compté, that are broken or lopsided, are melted down and reworked into more creamy pieces, as *crème de gruyère,* or sometimes *fondu.* This means "melted" and is not the same as *fondue.*

This cheese became so popular that the supply of injured wheels was not sufficient to meet the demand and now wheels are fabricated which, from the beginning, are intended for *fondu.*

Among the soft cheeses of the Jura are *Vacherin* and *Cancoillote,* a rather strong fromage. Just to add to the confusion, Cancoillote is not only the cheese itself, but a French type of Welsh Rabbit made from it. This pale yellow runny cheese is cooked with eggs and garlic.

In Eastern France Fondue is made with the Comté cheese, melted in white wine, with a touch of kirsch added at the finish. It is served at the table piping hot in a wooden bowl which has been rubbed inside with a clove of garlic. Eaters follow the Swiss custom of stabbing a crusty square of bread with the fork, swirling it around in the pot then lifting the soaked tidbit to the mouth.

Only dry white wine should be drunk with the fondue, tradition insists, although I know a girl who loved to upset tradition by drinking red wine with her fondue—claiming it was okay because she was color-blind. In Switzerland the custom is to drink Fendant, but in France almost any dry white wine of the region is not disdained.

This is the fondue formula recommended by the Switzerland Cheese Association.

(The elegant Hotel Plaza-Athénée, over on the Right Bank in Paris, serves it as La Fondue Savoyarde, or Fondue Neuf-Châtel.)

FONDUE NEUCHATELOISE
[Serves 4]

1 pound Switzerland Swiss cheese, shredded or fine-cut
3 tablespoons flour
1 clove fresh garlic, sliced in half
2 cups dry white wine (preferably Neuchâtel, Fendant, Riesling or Chablis)
1 tablespoon lemon juice
5 tablespoons kirsch or 4 tablespoons brandy
Nutmeg, fresh-ground pepper or páprika to taste
2 loaves French or Italian bread

Dredge cheese lightly with flour.

Rub coquelin (round, casserole-type earthenware pot with handle) or heavy metal fondue pot, with cut clove of garlic. Pour in wine and set over very low heat. (Fondue is best made over alcohol stove with adjustable flame or electric plate with asbestos pad that will hold utensil securely.) When air bubbles rise to surface of wine, add lemon juice. Stir with wooden fork or spoon and add the cheese by handfuls, melting each completely before adding another and stirring constantly.

Keep stirring until mixture starts bubbling lightly. Add kirsch and seasonings, stirring until blended.

Serve bubbling hot. A preheated chafing dish may be used. Cut loaves of bread into bite-sized pieces, each with at least one crust side. Spear bread through soft part first, securing points of wooden fork in crust, so you will not lose bread in pot.

Dunk in fondue in a stirring motion, swirling in fondue to get bread well saturated. The stirring will help maintain proper consistency of fondue.

Keep fondue simmering or bubbling lightly by regulating heat or turning on and off. If it becomes too thick, stir in enough pre-heated wine to thin to proper consistency.

Toward end, some of melted cheese will form a brown

crust at bottom of pot. Then lower heat to prevent pot
from cracking; lift out crust with fork and share this
delicacy with whoever is still able to eat.

Variations: Fondue Half and Half: Use ½ pound of
Switzerland Swiss (Emmentaler) and ½ pound Gruyère,
as many Swiss hotel and innkeepers do.

Fondue Gruyère: Use all natural Gruyère in place of
Swiss for a slightly sharper fondue.

Various Dunkers: Instead of bread, try cooked shrimp,
cooked cocktail frankfurters, tiny cooked meat balls,
popcorn, cut-up hard rolls, etc.

From Barbara Watkins in Paris: "I spent a week one
time with a Swiss family at Neuchâtel. They had one
of the famous fondues one evening and believe me it was
quite a ceremony—the fondue in the middle of the table
in the chafing dish; all of us armed with long forks
would, upon signal, stand up and plunge our breaded-
forks into the steaming cheese. Then, this was almost
washed down with a glass of Neuchâtel wine—sort of like
the Russians with their vodka following their caviar
snacks. We didn't have to sing the national anthem but
just short of that. Then I was told that the best part was
the sort of crusty portion stuck around the inside edges of
the chafing dish, so I was allowed this as the V.I.P."

In many a restaurant in Switzerland there is a *Fondue
Stubli* (little fondue room) that specializes in the serving
and eating of the cheese variety of fondue. Now, the way
it is prepared at the Horseshoe Grill of the Schwartzer-
hof Hotel in Berne is this:

BERNE FONDUE
[Serves 4]

1 teaspoon salt	Salt to taste
1 cut clove garlic	¼ teaspoon nutmeg
½ bottle dry white wine	1 tablespoon potato flour or
2 cups diced Gruyère cheese	cornstarch
2 cups diced Emmentaler	2 tablespoons kirsch
cheese	Cubes of lightly-toasted
	French bread

In heavy coquelin or earthenware casserole, place 1 teaspoon salt. Rub cut ends of garlic into salt until you can't any more. Pour in wine and heat to a boil. Add cheeses a little at a time, stirring constantly until each batch melts.

Lower heat by half; add more salt to taste and the nutmeg.

Make paste of potato flour and 1 tablespoon of the kirsch. Add to coquelin and continue stirring until thickened and smooth. Add remaining tablespoon of kirsch and blend in.

Serve to guests with basket of bread cubes. Also serve chilled white wine during and a thimble of kirsh after.

Jean Combe, *patron* of Le Dezaley, near Zurich, serves this

FONDUE FOR TWO

1 split clove garlic	1½ cups grated Emmentaler cheese
3 cups very dry wine	
1¼ cups grated Gruyère cheese	2 teaspoons potato flour
	4 tablespoons kirsch
Salt and pepper	

Rub inside of coquelin or other fondue pot with garlic, which is then discarded.

Pour wine into pot and cook to boiling. Stir in cheeses a bit at a time, stirring gently until cheese melts and combines with wine.

Mix and blend potato flour with the kirsch. Stir this into the hot mixture. Add salt and pepper to taste and cook to a slow boil. If done in kitchen, bring to table over alcohol or Sterno burner.

Dip crusty bread impaled on fondue forks into pot, swirl until saturated and eat with care.

Generous quantities of chilled dry white wine can accompany this fondue. In addition, each one has a couple ounces of kirsch in a glass. Midway through the fondue, half the kirsch is tossed off. Other half is drunk when fondue is almost finished.

Meal is concluded with cup of hot, black tea, flavored with Pflumli (prunelle brandy).

Cornelia Meili, of Zurich and Seattle, a home economist and member of the American Women's Club of Switzerland, is responsible for

FONDUE GENEVA
[Serves 4]

8 egg yolks	Pinch grated nutmeg
2 cups Gruyère cheese, grated	Pinch salt
	5 ounces butter
Pinch pepper	½ cup cream

Fried bread or noodles

In saucepan or fondue pot over gentle flame mix egg yolks, cheese, pepper, nutmeg and salt; stir continuously without boiling. Add the butter, bit by bit, still stirring. When mixture thickens, add cream, stir a little longer and invite guests to start dipping forkfuls of fried bread.

In Geneva this dish is often served on individual heated plates over hot noodles.

SIMPLE SWISS FONDUE
[Serves 4]

1 pound Emmentaler cheese, in small dice	½ bottle dry white wine
	2 ounces kirsch
1 tablespoon butter	1 teaspoon dry mustard

In earthenware fondue pot heat cheese and butter, stirring continuously until melted. Keep stirring and add wine gradually. More stirring as you add kirsch. Continue to stir while adding mustard. When smooth and slightly bubbling, start dipping chunks of bread in, on fondue forks.

A non-alcoholic fondue from the Switzerland Cheese Association, which boasts: "Anyone can make the holes . . . only the Swiss make the flavor."

TEENAGERS' FONTINA
[Serves 4]

2 tablespoons butter	1 pound Switzerland Swiss
4 tablespoons flour	cheese, grated
4 cups milk	Pinch salt
Pinch nutmeg	

In pot or skillet melt butter, add flour and stir over low heat until blended. Gradually add the milk, stirring. By handfuls add the cheese, then the salt and nutmeg. Stir until smooth.

Just below the Alps in the northern Italian province of Piedmont ("foot of the mountain") the great fondue specialty, in addition to Bagna Calda, is Fonduta, made with the Fontina cheese of the valley of Aosta, which is snuggled up against the mountains leading to Switzerland. To have the right-tasting Fonduta, you must use this Fontina d'Aosta, which *The Cheese Book* praises as "a cheese that belongs with the top dozen cheeses that are being made anywhere today." Fortunately, it is well distributed throughout the U. S. of A.

With the cheese settled, there comes the matter of other ingredients and method of preparation. As the result of a query I made among friends and other culinary sources for fondue recipes, I have 10 different ways to prepare Fonduta. Among them were 4 formulas from de luxe Italian hotels belonging to the C.I.G.A. chain and, where Hilton or Sheraton hotels in this country would have standardized recipes, these were very individual. So were the ones from Luigi Carnacina, the dean of Italian food experts; Marina Deserti of the Bologna food specialty family; the fashion designers, the Fontana sisters, and Mrs. Paola Lucentini of New York who has been helping me with translations for my monumental Italian cookbook.

I cannot bore you with 10 different Fonduta recipes.
So I will blend them, stirring constantly, into one which
will permit you to use your own judgment as to ingredients and method.

FLEXIBLE FONDUTA WITH WHITE TRUFFLES
[Serves 4 to 6]

2/3 to 1½ pounds Fontina cheese (or Gruyère, if not available)	White pepper to taste (so you will have no black pepper specks)
Milk, from "to cover" up to 1 quart ¹	4 to 8 tablespoons soft butter
Egg yolks, 3 to 12	1 4-ounce white Alba truffle, sliced very thin
Flour	

Toast

As Turin is in Piedmont, we begin with the method
of the *Excelsior Grand Hotel Principi di Piemonte.*
Cube cheese and soak in milk to cover (1 pint), in tall
narrow container for 30 minutes. (Some recipes call for
overnight soaking.)

Beat egg yolks (6) and incorporate 1 teaspoon flour,
blending to keep from lumping. Add softened cheese and
milk and place all in saucepan over very low heat (or
boiling water) and stir continuously until cheese is
melted and mixture is like velvety cream. It must cook
between a simmer and a boil, but never boil.

Remove from heat and add white pepper and butter
(4 tablespoons) in bits, blending well. Pour into fondue
pot and bring to table. Cover with paper-thin slices of
truffle. Dip in cubes of toast on fondue forks or fingers
of toast with fingers.

At the *Excelsior in Rome,* after soaking the cheese
(1⅓ pounds) in milk for 6 hours, the butter (⅓ pound)
is added along with 12 egg yolks and the cheese and the
milk, and all placed in top of double boiler over hot
water.

¹ The Hotel Danieli in Venice uses dry white wine or beer instead
of milk.

At the *Excelsior in Naples* (looking out at Vesuvius and Capri) after the milk soaking, cheese (1⅓ pounds), milk (5 ounces) and butter (3 ounces) are all simmered together, stirring with a wooden spatula until the cheese is all melted. Then the egg yolks (4) are added and "mingled accurately." As soon as Fonduta has achieved the consistency of thick cream, remove from heat, pour into fondue pot, sprinkle with slices of truffle and serve with small pieces of toast, fried in butter.

The *Hotel Danieli Royal Excelsior* (after all it is three buildings) in Venice uses 1 pound of Fontina melted with 4 tablespoons butter in top pot of double boiler over very hot water. Egg yolks are added to the number of 3, plus "some good wine or beer" to taste, stirring all the while. When smooth and creamy and ready for the table, taste for salt and pepper and add blades of truffle.

If the above choices throw you, here is a simple version sent to me by the Sorella Fontana of Rome and Bologna.

FONDUTA ALLA PIEMONTESE
[Serves 4]

½ pound first quality Fontina cheese	Salt
	2 egg yolks
1 cup scalded milk	2 tablespoons melted butter
1 large truffle, sliced thin	

Cut cheese into small pieces.

Pour ½ cup of the milk into upper half of double boiler, add cheese, a sprinkle of salt and cook over boiling water, stirring energetically until creamy. Add egg yolks which have been mixed with remaining milk and the butter and stir until the fondue results, clear and "shiny."

Pour into fondue pot or 4 ramekins and add the sliced truffle. Serve very warm. "Buon Appetito!"

Italian wines to accompany Fonduta? Try Soave from the Romeo and Juliet country; Verdicchio, or Verdicchio dei Castelli di Jesi.

Proving there is little or nothing new under the sun, in the early 1800's, the godfather of fine-feeding writing, Brillat-Savarin, in a little essay on fondues gave a recipe which is very like our Fonduta.

Coming from Belley (how appropriate can you get?) near the Swiss border of France, he knew what he was writing about when he said "it originated in Switzerland. . . . It is a wholesome, savory and appetising dish, and being quickly cooked, is always useful when guests arrive unexpectedly."

BRILLAT-SAVARIN'S ORIGINAL FONDUE AU FROMAGE

Weigh the number of eggs you want to use for your guests (1, 2 or 3 per person). Medium to large eggs weigh about 2 ounces each.

Take a piece of good Gruyère cheese which weighs ⅓ the weight of the eggs and a piece of butter weighing ⅙ the weight of the eggs.

Break the eggs into a pan and beat them thoroughly, then add the cheese, either shredded or thin-sliced, and mix in the butter.

Place the pan over hot water (double boiler or chafing dish) and stir with a wooden spoon or spatula until mixture is thick and softish.

If the cheese is old, no salt is required; if new/fresh, salt to taste. In any case, pepper it handsomely.

Serve on hot buttered toast.

This is an old English recipe, courtesy Capt. Scarritt Adams, U.S.N. Ret., of Bermuda. As you can tell by comparing, it borrows much from Brillat-Savarin.

FONDUE OF CHEESE

When there is no handsome Stilton or Cottenham to present, or it is wished to avoid the break in a dinner caused by "the cheese course" (of which few may care to partake, and which the few that do care to partake, decline, to avoid being singular), some sort of cheese in a cooked or melted form forms a most agreeable substitute.

Weigh in their shells the eggs you mean to use.

Take the third of their weight of grated white cheese (Gruyère is the best, but good English kinds will do) and a sixth of that weight in butter. Break the eggs into a saucepan and mix with them the butter and cheese, seasoning rather highly with pepper and slightly with salt.

Set the saucepan on the fire and stir the whole together until the eggs are set, keeping it light.

Then turn it out on a hot dish, and serve instantaneously, sending around with it the mustard-pot.

FONDUE ITALIANO
[Serves 4]

1 clove garlic, split
1 cup Soave, Verdicchio or dry Orvieto or Frascati wine
½ pound Fontina cheese, diced (2 cups)
¼ pound Parmesan cheese, grated (1 cup)
1½ teaspoons potato flour
1 teaspoon oregano
Salt and fresh-ground pepper
2 tablespoons Marsala wine

Rub wooden stirring spoon and inside of fondue pot with garlic. Place over low heat with 1 cup wine inside and heat to simmer. Add cheeses and stir continuously until melted and blended with wine.

Make paste of potato flour and a little cold water and blend into cheese-wine mixture. Season with oregano and salt and pepper to taste. Add Marsala and invite guests to dip in crusty bits of Italian bread.

FONTINA FONDUE
[Serves 4]

1 8-ounce can tomato sauce with mushrooms
2 cups shredded Fontina (or Muenster) cheese
1 tablespoon flour
1 6-ounce can evaporated milk
½ teaspoon onion salt
⅛ teaspoon garlic salt or powder
⅛ teaspoon oregano

Bring tomato sauce to boil in saucepan; reduce heat to simmer.

Dredge cheese in flour; add to sauce. After cheese is melted, add evaporated milk gradually, stirring until smooth. Add seasonings and stir.

Transfer to fondue pot at table, keep hot and use breadsticks or squares of crusty Italian (or French) bread for dipping.

Marina Deserti, of the firm that handles the Escoffier products in Italy, spells it "Bagna Caoda" and the chef at the *Excelsior Grand Hotel Principi di Piemonte* in Turin and several other authorities write "Bagna Cauda," but in any case it means "hot bath" and it is the Piedmont hot dip for vegetables.

There it is popular in the season when they harvest cardoons, or white edible thistles. Here we can use a number of other more available raw vegetables (listed at the end of the recipe, which I've "consolidated" from the several sent me from Italy).

BAGNA CALDA
[Makes 1½ cups]

¼ pound (1 stick) sweet butter	2 tablespoons anchovy paste
3 cloves garlic [1]	1 white truffle [3]
1 cup olive oil [2]	Pinch salt
	Dash cayenne pepper

---

[1] Marina Deserti: "In the Belbo Valley, they chop the garlic very much, after having let it soak for 2 hours in milk, to take off the reek and make it more digestible."

[2] Marina Deserti: "In the old times they used walnut oil, that cannot be found now. To have that old traditional taste, you may crush some walnut kernels in the mixture."

I found walnut oil for sale in Macy's in New York, at around $2.50 a pint. Excellent, but at that price maybe you better pound 4 walnut halves in a mortar and add to olive oil.

[3] Optional. White truffles from Italy may be purchased at gourmet shops and Italian groceries, usually one to a can. Do not be put off by their smell when can is opened—they really add something when cooked in the Bagna Calda. Either thin-slice them or mince them for this dish.

In fondue pot melt butter over very low flame; add garlic and let it cook without browning. Add oil in thin stream, almost drop by drop, blending well.

Remove from heat and stir in anchovy paste, dissolving it completely. Add truffle, salt and cayenne.

Replace over low heat and bring up to simmer, but do not boil. Dip vegetables in, each guest doing his own.

Vegetables for Bagna Calda

Young scallions or green onions

White leaves of savoy cabbage, coarsely shredded

Cauliflower flowerets

Strips of pimiento, sweet red, yellow, or green pepper

Cucumber, peeled, seeded and in strips

Young carrots, scraped and in strips

Celery stalks or strips

Jerusalem artichokes

JANE FONDUE
[Serves 4 to 6]

2 ounces sliced white truffles

2 cups Asti Spumante (or pink champagne)

½ pound Fontina cheese, diced

½ pound Bel Paese cheese, diced

4 tablespoons flour

2 egg yolks

Suspicion of Tabasco sauce

White pepper to taste

Warm truffles in 1¾ cups of the Spumante in fondue pot on range over medium heat. Add cheeses which have been dredged with the flour. Stir with wooden spoon until smooth.

Beat egg yolks with remaining ¼ cup of Spumante. Stir into fondue mixture and blend well. Blend in Tabasco and white pepper and when bubbling transfer pot to warmer on table. Dip in squares of brioche, croissants cut crosswise in segments, or other high-class breads.

White pepper is simply black pepper with the black hulls removed.

Here is a recipe from the popular Wilshire Boulevard Restaurant in Los Angeles.

LA FONDA FONDUE
[Serves 4 to 6]

1 1-pound can refried beans	Cheddar cheese,
1 8-ounce can tomato sauce	shredded
with onions	¼ teaspoon garlic salt or
4 ounces Monterey Jack or	powder

½ teaspoon chili powder

Combine all ingredients in earthenware fondue pot over medium heat and cook, stirring, until cheese melts and mixture is hot.

Transfer to burner on table and serve with Fritos, tostados or hot cocktail frankfurters.

Perhaps the greatest influence on American cooking were the restaurants of the Delmonico family. They came from Switzerland and introduced fine French cooking to the American palate. One of the many dishes they brought dates from the 1880's but I saw it first recorded 10 years later.

DELMONICO 1893 FONDUE
[Serves 4]

1 pound soft, fresh Swiss	2 tablespoons milk
cheese	4 tablespoons Piedmontese
12 egg yolks	truffles (or white mush-
2 tablespoons flour	rooms), peeled and finely
1 pint cream	minced

1 tablespoon butter

Cut cheese into ¼-inch squares.

Break egg yolks into bowl, add flour, beat and mix well together; dilute with cream. Strain through a sieve.

Put cheese in saucepan on a slow fire with milk; stir it about with wooden spoon until it no longer forms into strings. Then pour in prepared yolks. Heat all on the fire, stirring it about with spoon until it assumes consistency of a cream (but it must not boil).

Add butter and 3 tablespoons truffles. Pour all into fondue casserole and sprinkle top with remaining 1 tablespoon truffles.

RABBIT FONDUE
[Serves 4]

2 tablespoons butter	Dash cayenne
1 pound sharp Cheddar or Gruyère cheese, shredded	1 teaspoon Worcestershire sauce
½ teaspoon dry mustard	½ cup beer or ale
½ teaspoon salt	2 eggs, barely beaten
	Thick toast in 1-inch squares

Melt butter in pan or skillet; add cheese and heat, stirring until melted.

Pour into fondue pot over medium heat; add mustard, salt, cayenne, and Worcestershire, blend well.

Mix the beer with the eggs and add to pot, cooking until thicker, stirring frequently.

Dunk toast, speared on wooden forks or skewers.

Here is a hare of a different color.

ANOTHER RABBIT FONDUE
[Serves 4]

¼ cup butter or margarine	1½ teaspoons Worcestershire sauce
¼ cup flour	7 tablespoons catsup
½ teaspoon salt	2 cups (½ pound) sharp Cheddar cheese, shredded
¼ teaspoon dry mustard	
1 12-ounce can beer or ale	

Melt butter in saucepan; blend in flour, salt and dry mustard. Gradually stir in beer; add Worcestershire and catsup. Cook, stirring constantly, until mixture thickens and comes to a boil. Add cheese and cook, stirring constantly, until cheese has melted.

Transfer to fondue pot at table.

Serve with chunks of pumpernickel bread.

FARMER'S FONDUE
[Serves 4]

2 cups cubed Herkimer,
   Cornhusker, or other
   sharp Cheddar cheese
4 ounces (1 stick) butter

6 eggs, well beaten
Paprika, cayenne,
   fresh-ground pepper, salt

Over low heat, melt cheese, add butter and cook together with eggs until mixture is thick and smooth, stirring constantly. Add seasonings to taste and blend together. Do not let it come to a boil.

Teress Altschul, who paints lovely pictures of children, contributes

NEVER-FAIL CHEESE FONDUE
[Serves 4]

Clove garlic, cut
½ pound Emmentaler
   cheese, grated
¼ pound Gruyère cheese,
   grated
¼ pound Tilsit cheese,
   grated

1¼ cups dry Chablis
3 tablespoons cornstarch
4 tablespoons kirsch
Dash fresh-ground pepper
Sprinkle nutmeg
French bread in bite-sized
   squares

Rub pot with garlic; add grated cheeses and heat slowly.

In another pan, heat wine to below boiling point. Pour over cheese and stir with wooden spoon over low heat.

Mix cornstarch in kirsch and add to pot, stirring until mixture is smooth. Add pepper and nutmeg. Adjust burner under pot so it bubbles slightly.

Have the French bread ready. It is best when the cut chunks are permitted to dry overnight.

The following is a somewhat different recipe which results in a hot dip for the raw vegetables listed, as well as cooked artichoke leaves.

CREAMY FONDUE
[Serves 4]

4 tablespoons butter	1 cup grated Parmesan
2 tablespoons flour	cheese
1½ cups Chablis, Graves, or	3 tablespoons sour cream
Sauternes	½ teaspoon oregano
1 cup cubed Muenster	Pinch paprika
cheese	

In saucepan, melt butter, stir in flour and continue stirring and blending over low heat until mixture is fairly dry. Add wine, ½ cup at a time, blending with wire whisk until each addition is integrated. Then add cheeses, a handful at a time, and stir until each batch is melted before adding next. Stir in sour cream, oregano and sprinkle with paprika.

Pour into fondue pot and bring to table over medium heat. Dip or dunk vegtables in this creamy mixture.

Young Raw Vegetables for Dunking

Leaves of

Red, green, white cabbage	Dandelion
Spinach	Young nasturtium
Tender, inner celery	Mustard and cress

Whole

Small mushrooms	Red radishes
New carrots	Cauliflowerets
Runner beans	Heart of celery
Tiny red and yellow tomatoes	

Strips of

Cabbage heart	Green, yellow and red sweet
Carrots	pepper
White radishes	Celery

For those unexpected occasions when guests drop in without warning at mealtime or midnight, have on hand these ingredients, duck into the kitchen a few minutes and come out bearing a fondue pot and heat source to offer an almost magical table-top treat.

FAST FONDUE
[Serves 4]

½ pound sharp cheese	1 can evaporated milk
(American, Cheddar,	1 egg, slightly beaten
Emmentaler, etc.)	¼ teaspoon dry or prepared
chopped in bits	mustard to taste
Salt and pepper to taste	

In double boiler over very hot water cook cheese in milk, stirring until cheese melts and blends. Remove from heat and stir in egg, mustard and seasonings; mix thoroughly.

Bring to table in fondue pot and serve with crackers or cubes of bread, to be dunked.

Faith and Mac Miller have given me this recipe which stretches or contracts, according to the number (and size) of your guests.

FLEXIBLE FONDUE
[Serves 4]

1 pint dry white wine	cheese
2 cloves garlic	Flour
1 pound imported Swiss	Sprinkle fresh-grated nutmeg

Put wine and garlic in fondue pot over lowish heat or in top of double boiler over boiling water and bring to a boil.

Grate cheese and bounce in a brown paper bag with flour to coat. Then very slowly dribble cheese into the hot wine. Stir this slowly and constantly. This should take 20 minutes, or a martini and a half's time . . . till the whole mess is the consistency of very soft putty. Add nutmeg while stirring. Invite eaters to dip walnut-sized chunks of French bread and wind the fondue around their forks.

This recipe at the ratio of a pint of wine to a pound of cheese serves 4. But for larger or smaller appetites, it can be doubled or halved.

This and any light salad is *a meal.*

C.M.U. FONDUE
[Serves 4]

1 cup Edam or Kuminost cheese, chopped	diced
1 cup Roquefort or Gorgonzola cheese, crumbled	1 cup Emmentaler or Cheddar cheese, diced
	3 tablespoons flour
	2 cups dry white wine
1 cup Muenster with cumin, or other spiced cheese,	3 tablespoons dry vermouth
	1 tablespoon lemon juice

Fresh-ground pepper, nutmeg or paprika to taste

Combine cheese bits in paper bag with flour and shake well to coat each piece.

Heat wine in fondue pot until small bubbles appear. Add cheeses, a little at a time, until all are melted, stirring with wooden spoon in one direction. Do not heat too high or cheese will become stringy. Add vermouth, lemon juice and one of the seasonings. Dunk as usual.

C.M.U.? It stands for "crazy mixed up."

FONDUE FOR ONE

1 egg	1 tablespoon Gruyère cheese, grated
Salt and pepper	
	1 teaspoon butter

Beat egg in small saucepan with a little salt and plenty of fresh-ground pepper. Cut butter into bits and add it and cheese to egg.

Place pan over high heat and keep stirring mixture until it thickens enough to eat with a fork. Take off at once, place on warmed dish and serve (yourself, no doubt).

MIXED FONDUE
[Serves 6 to 8]

2 cups cubed Emmentaler cheese	1 tablespoon lemon juice Fresh-ground pepper
2 cups cubed Gruyère cheese	3 tablespoons kirsch
3 tablespoons flour	½ pound little cooked beefballs
1 clove garlic, split	½ pound cubed cooked ham
2 cups dry white wine	French bread

In paper bag, toss cheese cubes and flour.

Rub interior of fondue pot and stirring spoon with garlic, then discard.

Place wine in pot, heat until small bubbles appear around edge; add lemon juice. Add floured cheese a handful at a time, stirring until each melts. Keep stirring until mixture is creamy and barely simmering. Season to taste with pepper, add kirsch and mix well. Heat to bubbling.

If pot has been heated on kitchen stove, transfer to table and keep simmered. If cooked in saucepan, transfer to fondue pot which has been warmed with hot water.

Diners get assortment of bread cubes, beefballs and ham which they skewer and dip into pot and coat with cheese mixture.

CROQUE VINCENT
[Serves 1]

1 slice sandwich bread
Butter
1 slice Mozzarella cheese
1 small veal cutlet

Salt and pepper
Lemon juice
1 slice prosciutto (or very thin
slice Virginia ham)

Flour

Butter bread lightly and lay on it slice of cheese to fit.

Pound veal cutlet very thin, cut to fit bread, season on both sides with salt and pepper and wet with lemon juice, then dust lightly with flour. Cut prosciutto the size of bread slice.

In blazer pan melt 1½ tablespoons butter and bring to point where it sizzles but does not smoke. Lay in veal and prosciutto and brown quickly on one side. Turn over, put ham on top of veal, then cheese on ham and bread over all. Reduce heat and cook another couple of minutes, until second side of veal is golden.

Put 1 tablespoon butter in pan. When it melts, use a spatula to turn the whole sandwich over. Cook until bread is crisp and golden brown. By this time cheese will be melty. Remove to warm plate and serve at once.

RACLETTE

The No. 2 cheese dish of Switzerland. After a large Gruyère cheese is cut in two, the cut side of one of the halves is placed alongside a hot, preferably wood or charcoal, fire. As the surface melts, it is scraped off onto a plate and eaten with boiled white onions, potatoes and pickles.

In restaurants serving Raclette in Switzerland you can have all you can eat, but more than nine servings will probably draw an audience.

ROQUEFORT RACLETTE
[Serves 8 to 10]

1½-wheel (3 pounds) Roquefort cheese

Salt and fresh-ground pepper

2 sliced loaves French bread

Place cheese in refrigerator 8 hours or overnight. Remove and place on heavy aluminum foil or baking pan under broiler, with more foil under both ends so that cut side is parallel with source of heat, and 3 inches below. Broil briefly, until top is soft and melted. Remove and scrape off melted part and spread on slices of French bread. Season to taste.

Return cheese to broiler and repeat, melting and scraping rest of cheese, raising cheese as it gets thinner, so that top is always 3 inches from heat. Begin serving as soon as first scraping is spread.

ELECTRIC FONDUES

Remember Ramona, the virtuoso electric organist? Well, she's now Mrs. Robert Sutton of Laguna Miguel, California, and she sent me the following letter:

"I got an electric fondue dish for Christmas and we love it! No mess, no fuss and great for beef. A suggestion for cheese fondue, etc. when doing it with an electric fondue set: use a different pot, otherwise it messes up the dish for beef. I have a special colorful dish for cheese and use the original pan for beef.

"With the beef we serve chopped peanuts, sour cream and chives, mayonnaise and curry, homemade red chili sauce and cottage cheese, plus spinach salad and hot rolls.

"For dessert we like hot apple pie and cheese. And thin chocolate mints with our coffee."

CLASSIC SWISS FONDUE
[Serves 4 to 6 as main dish; 8 to 12 as appetizer]

2 cups dry white wine
  (Chablis, Moselle, dry
  Sauterne or Rhine)
1 pound natural Swiss
  cheese, cubed
3 tablespoons kirsch

3 tablespoons cornstarch
½ clove garlic
  Dash each, white pepper,
  paprika, nutmeg
⅛ teaspoon baking soda
1 loaf French bread, in
  1-inch cubes

Heat wine in electric fondue pot until bubbles begin to rise to surface.

Put cheese, kirsch, cornstarch, garlic, and seasonings into blender container, add heated wine, cover and process at high (liquefy) until smooth.

Pour into fondue pot and cook over medium heat, stirring constantly, until mixture is heated and bubbly. Add baking soda and mix well. Reduce heat to maintain slight bubbling during serving. Dip in bread cubes.

Morrison Wood, the wine and food sachem, recommends as the kirsch you use, Swiss Kirsch Dettling Superior Vieux—if you can get it.

Instead of kirsch, substitute other fruit liqueurs or brandies, or light rum.

In Minnesota, they rub the pot with garlic, throw in wine, cheese and cornstarch together, slowly stir and bring *almost* to a boil, add kirsch—and eat.

ELECTRIC VARIATIONS FOR CLASSIC SWISS CHEESE FONDUES

Onion-Cheese Fondue: Add 1 envelope (about 1½ ounces) onion soup mix to the wine before heating. Omit salt and nutmeg.

Fondue with Ham or Canadian Bacon: Stir in 1 cup fine-chopped, fully-cooked ham or Canadian bacon just before serving.

Fondue with Mushrooms: Stir in 1 or 2 4½-ounce cans mushrooms, drained and fine-chopped, just before serving. Try adding 2 teaspoons fine-chopped chives for added zest.

Shrimp Fondue: Add 1 or 2 4½-ounce cans drained and fine-chopped shrimp before serving.

Caraway Fondue: Use ½ pound Swiss cheese mixed with ½ pound Caraway seed cheese.

Truffle Fondue: Chop truffles and sauté them in a little hot butter. Add when fondue is ready to be served.

Flaming Fondue: For splendid serving: Heat ¼ cup kirsch in a ladle and pour over the bubbling fondue. Flame it, and begin to dunk when flame has died down.

From Rosemary Cartwright who formerly lived in Rome: "A Roman friend did a Cheese Fondue perhaps better than most, due to the addition of rum."

This is a suggestion that the experimental fondue-ist may adopt and tinker with. While results are not guaranteed, a lot of carefree reaction is bound to result. You might let me know results for our next edition, if you are clear-headed enough to jot down ingredients, measurements, and methods.

AMERICAN FONDUE
[Serves 5 or 6 as main dish; 10 to 12 as appetizer]

½ package dry onion soup mix
¼ cup warm water
¼ cup butter (½ stick)
2 cups milk

1 pound American or Cheddar cheese, cubed
1 2-ounce jar pimientos, drained and chopped
¼ cup flour

Soak onion soup mix in water 5 minutes.

Heat butter and milk in electric fondue pot over high heat until butter melts.

Put soup mix and water, cheese, pimientos and flour into blender container; add hot milk and butter, cover and turn on high until smooth.

Pour into fondue pot and cook over medium heat,

stirring frequently, until thickened. Reduce heat so fondue bubbles slightly during serving.

For dipping: French or Italian bread chunks, corn chips, small toast squares.

Mice, say the rodent researchers, really don't love cheese. They will settle for a bit of *fromage* if nothing else tastier is available, but their real passion, gastronomically speaking, is divided between bacon and gumdrops.

FOODS TO DUNK AND DIP IN CHEESE FONDUES

Breads

French and Italian	Hard and soft rolls
Rye and wholewheat	Rye and pumpernickel rolls
	English muffins

Cut into 1-inch cubes with at least 1 side crusted. May be toasted before or after cutting.

Fruits and Vegetables

Apples	Small mushrooms
Pears	Green onions
Cauliflowerets (see directions	Green peppers, in strips
p. 28)	Sweet red peppers, in strips
Celery sticks	Potatoes, boiled
Cucumber sticks	Cherry tomatoes
	Zucchini strips

Cut apple, pear and potatoes in bite-sized cubes. Dip others by hand.

Meat and Seafood

Ham	Fresh shrimp
Frankfurters	King crab
Cocktail franks	Lobster

Precook and cut into bite-size pieces. Foods may be warmed on tray before serving.

Snack Foods

Potato and corn chips	Crackers and biscuits
	Pizza wedges

Serve in colorful bowl and dip with fingers.

Rule to Remember: Keep the Cheese Fondue stirred so it won't thicken at bottom of pot.

A DIRECTORY OF CHEESES
FOR FONDUES

These are most of the cheeses available in the United States for making fondues. They were selected for their meltability and availability.

While a number may be difficult to find in the limited cases of grocery and dairy stores, almost all can be purchased in cheese specialty shops—and all are available at such emporia as Cheeses of all Nations, 153 Chambers Streeet, New York, N.Y. 10007; Cheese Village, 3 Greenwich Ave., N.Y. 10014; and Cheese Unlimited, 1263 Lexington Ave., New York, N.Y. 10028. These three establishments do a mail order business to anywhere in the continental United States.

Large department stores with food departments (such as Macy's and Bloomingdale's in Manhattan) also have extensive selections of cheeses. So does William Poll, 1051 Lexington Ave.

AMERICAN: Same as Cheddar. Comes "natural," "processed," "processed cheese food" and "spread." Only the natural is recommended, as the others contain fillers, chemicals, etc. which interfere with the melting process, with the result that the "cheese" becomes stringy, like plastic, or refuses to melt. A great many American eaters know of no other cheese but this manufactured and manipulated gunk, mainly because it comes in convenient sandwich-slice form and, due to addition of preservatives, it keeps well.

APPENZELLER: A Swiss made in Canton of Appenzell, made usually from skim cow's milk, sometimes whole; soaked in cider or white wine and spices. Zesty, nut-like.

ASADERO: Also called Oaxaca, white, whole-milk Mex-

ican. Melts easily. Asadero: "fit for roasting." Originated in state of Oaxaca, now mostly made in Jalisco.

ASIAGO: Originated in town of that name in Vicenza,
Italy. From cow's milk. Hard, zesty, grated and mixed
with other cheeses for fondues, or sprinkled like Parmesan.

BATTELMATT: Nutty, sharp Swiss, made in Canton of
Tessin; softer and moister than Emmentaler.

BEAUFORT: Cow's milk, harder than Gruyère, from Savoie. Recommended by A. Cochet of Au Savoyard in
Pairs, ½ and ½ Gruyère for the perfect fondue.

BEL PAESE: "Beautiful country." Trade name of popular
Italian table cheese. Soft, sweet, mild, smooth, mellow.
Usually a dessert cheese but can be combined with
other, harder cheeses for melting. Map on label tells
you if it is made in Italy or is domestic.

BITTO: Italian, from Lombardy; firm Swiss-type; similar
to Fontina and Montasio, from cow's milk; mixture
cow's and goat; or ewe's milk, skimmed or whole.
Nutty, zesty, best grated for melting.

BLARNEY: Ireland's answer to Emmentaler—and a fairly
faint echo.

CAERPHILLY: Made and popular in Wales; semi-soft,
cow's milk; white, smooth, granular.

CANTAL, also known locally as FOURME: A hard, yellow
cheese with piquant flavor and firm, close body. Made
for centuries in region of Auvergne Mountains, Dept.
of Cantal, France. The French cheese that most resembles Cheddar. But since it varies in flavor, taste before
buying.

CHEDDAR: Originally made in Somersetshire village of
Cheddar; first cheese factory in U.S. was Jesse Wil-
liams' in 1851 at Rome, N.Y. About 1½ billion
pounds now made annually in U.S., making it by far
the most popular. Also known as American and American Cheddar. Variations include Black Diamond
Cheddar, Cherry Hill Cheddar, Smoked Cheddar,
Cheddar Français, Irish, Australian, Canadian, Canadian Cheddar and Rum, Port Wine Cheddar Spread,
Czechoslovakian, English Farmhouse, Minor Aged,
New Zealand, Queso de Papa (Puerto Rico), Scottish;
and from U.S., California, Daisy, Illinois mellow and

sharp, Kentucky mellow and sharp, Minnesota mellow, Minnesota Sharpy, Natural Longhorn, New England Rat Cheese, Atomic from Ohio, sharp; Ohio State mellow, Rocky Mountain Blacky, Young American, Wisconsin Longhorn, medium sharp, sharp.

CHESHIRE: Also called Chester, first made at village of Chester on River Dee; said to have been originally molded in shape of famous Cheshire Cat. Like Cheddar but more crumbly; mellow, smooth; semi-hard.

COLBY: Similar to Cheddar; made in Australia, Belgium, New Zealand, Scotland and Sweden, in addition to U.S. Has softer body and more moisture than Cheddar. One of the cheeses I enjoy the most.

COMTÉ: Made in Franche-Comté, Jura Mountains of eastern France, resembles Gruyère, with little holes. Basis for a prepared fondue sold in U.S.

COON: A Cheddar cured by a special patented method; dark rind, white inside; crumbly, with sharp, tangy flavor.

CORNHUSKER: Introduced in Nebraska over 30 years ago. Similar to Cheddar and Colby, but softer and moister. A "rat-trap" cheese.

DANBO, DANISH EXPORT: Plain and seeded with caraway; mellow, made with skim milk and buttermilk; shaped like Gouda.

DERBY: Made in Derbyshire from cow's whole milk; similar to Cheddar but more flaky and moister; zesty and firm when it matures. SAGE DERBY, with sage leaves.

DORSET: Semi-hard, use grated; zesty and smooth, blend a little with Cheddar to add flavor; blue-veined.

DUNLOP: Rich, white, made in Scotland; resembles Cheddar.

EDAM: The mild, mellow, younger type can be cooked. Dutch, imported, but also made in U.S. Between 8 and 9 pounds of cheese is obtained from 100 pounds of milk.

EMMENTALER: Named after Emme Valley, Canton of Berne, where it originated. This is what is usually sold as Swiss cheese. Has large holes or eyes, because it "rises" similarly to bread; has hazel nut or walnut flavor and ripe, strong smell when aged, though wheels imported to U.S. are mild. But 80 years ago at U.S. free lunch counters it exuded most pungent aroma. Made here in Wisconsin and Ohio, quite good; brought in from Finland and sold as "Imported Swiss," but no word as to country of origin; a mild Emmentaler comes from Austria and Blarney from Ireland is just that. Samsoë is the Danish version.

ESTROM: Rich, soft Danish, Port Salut type. Very pleasing.

FLANDERS: A mellow Gouda type, from Belgium.

FONDUE CANCOILLOTTE: A combination of cheese products from north-east France eaten fresh there or canned and found in U.S. cheese stores. When heated and wine is added, makes an unusual fondue.

FONDUE DE CONSERVE: From the same district, a product of skim milk with crumbled bread, heated, salted and molded. Keeps well. With addition of boiling milk, butter, salt and pepper and sometimes egg yolks, it becomes a fondue.

FONDUE FROMAGE: Grated Gruyère, Comté and French Emmentaler, blended, ready to add wine and kirsch. 1 pound serves 4 guests.

FONDUTTA: A fatter, softer version of Muenster, made in Wisconsin.

FONTINA: A great Italian cheese, made of ewe's milk in the Aosta Valley of Piedmont and the basis for the Italian fondue—Fonduta.

FYNBO: A rich cheese of the Samsoë family and Samsoë is the Danish Gruyère.

GERÔME, also known as GERARDMER: From Lorraine and nearby Switzerland. Soft, creamy, greenish tint.

DOUBLE GLOUCESTER: Similar to Cheddar but has slightly pungent flavor. Smooth velvet texture and beautiful golden color.

GOLD 'N' RICH: A bland American cheese halfway between Bel Paese and Muenster in flavor. Melts and cooks well.

GOUDA, plain and smoked: Should be mixed with other cheese in fondue. Has more fat than Edam.

GOUDA WITH KUMMEL SEEDS, flavored with light Burgundy wine: A blended cheese which can be used in combination with another for fondues.

GOURMANDAISE: Mellow white French cheese flavored with kirsch. Used in fondues, cut out or down on kirsch in recipe.

GRUYÈRE, also known as GROYER and VACHELIN: Named for village of Gruyère, Canton of Fribourg, Switzerland. With Emmentaler, the most important cheese for the making of fondue. Is darker, nuttier, sharper and has smaller holes than Emmentaler.

CRÈME DE GRUYÈRE: A soft, smooth Gruyère made in France.

NOISETTE DE GRUYÈRE: A smooth, delicate Gruyère made with nuts, in France.

GRUYÈRE WITH PISTACHIOS: A blended cheese made in New York, perfumed with Neuchâtel wine.

HAVARTI and HAVARTI SEEDED: Light yellow Danish cheese with distinctive flavor and numerous holes. Use fairly fresh. The seeded comes with caraway.

HERKIMER COUNTY: A Cheddar-type cheese made in New York State. Fairly dry and crumbly with sharp flavor.

HICKORY SMOKED: One of the Cheddars made in the U.S. Hard, good for fondues.

JARLSBERG: Norway's answer to Swiss. Nutty, delicate flavor; wide-eyed, well-textured, buttery.

DOMESTIC KASSERI: Tastes somewhere between Parmesan and Cheddar.

KUMINOST: Spiced with cumin and caraway seed, made from skim-milk in Scandinavian countries.

LANCASHIRE, PLAIN AND SAGE: Very good melting and toasting version of Cheddar made in Lancaster, England.

LEYDEN: Mellow, spiced Dutch cheese; will add a certain kick when blended with other cheese for fondue. DELFT is almost exactly the same.

LONGHORN: Made in Texas, Michigan, Wisconsin and now Minnesota; zesty, old-fashioned Cheddar.

MARIBO: An unusual Danish cheese with a haunting after-taste; semi-hard, smooth, zesty.

MAY: Made in U.S., mellow, soft Gouda type.

MICHIGAN PINCONICK: A sharp Cheddar.

MONTASIO: A hard Italian cheese, to be grated like Parmesan for fondues.

MONTEREY JACK: A California cheese made from goat's

milk, somewhat like Muenster but not so bland, with small holes. Excellent for melting.

MOUNTAIN: A new Gruyère type from Israel.

MOZZARELLA: For children's fondues made with milk; does not blend with wine. Care must be taken in cooking to keep it from going stringy.

MUENSTER or MÜNSTER: Made in Germany, France, Denmark, Switzerland, Norway and the U.S. A pleasing, semi-soft, bland cheese, very well adapted to fondues. Comes also with caraway seeds.

MUENSTER WALNUT SPREAD: Blended cheese made in New York, with nuts and perfumed with Chablis.

MUTSCHLI: A Swiss goat's milk cheese used for Raclette.

NEW ENGLND RAT: A sharp Cheddar.

NEW YORK STATE CHEDDAR: Both medium and medium-sharp Cheddars.

NEW YORK STATE CHEDDAR WITH CASHEWS: A blended spread cheese perfumed with white wine.

ONION: A firm cheese with onions for those who like onion flavor in their fondues.

PARMESAN: The classic Italian hard, grating cheese. Adds a zesty touch to fondues if mixed with other cheeses.

PEPPER and HOT PEPPER: Firm, spicy, peppery American cheeses.

PFISTER: Although made differently, classed in the same group with Swiss cheeses.

PINEAPPLE: Gets its name from its shape and color and surface but it is a well-cured Cheddar type cheese. Mellow.

PROVOLONE: Made all over Italy and in Wisconsin and Michigan. Mellow, smooth, white. Blend with a Swiss for fondues.

PROVOLONE WITH CHIANTI: A blended cheese spread made in New York City; melts easily.

PUMPKIN: Named for shape and color; sharp, dry, firm; between Cheddar and Muenster.

RACLETTE BAGNE: The scraping cheese used in making Raclette, the Swiss melted cheese dish. Also for table use and for fondues. From the Valais region of Switzerland.

REBLOCHON: Strong, smelly, soft, French, buttery, occasionally used for fondue.

REGGIANO: Similar to Parmesan and used in the same manner.

SAGE: An American cheese of the Cheddar family spiced with the herb.

SALAMI RAUCHER: Austrian version of Gouda, lightly smoked, with chunks of salami. Also made with ham, and plain.

SAMSOË: Danish version of Swiss Emmentaler.

SAPSAGO: Small, hard cheese from Switzerland with powdered clover leaves. Used grated and in that form an unusual addition to fondues.

SARDO: A hard Italian grating cheese used like Parmesan.

SWISS: The over-all name for Emmentaler, made in Switzerland and exported as "Switzerland Swiss." Copies are made in the U.S., France, Denmark, Germany, Italy, Austria, Finland, Russia, and Argentina.

TILLAMOOK: A tasty Cheddar made in the Pacific Northwest and Colorado.

TILSITER: A North German and Central European soft, smelly cheese with a distinctive taste, sometimes spiced with caraway seeds.

TYBO: Partly skim milk, like Edam; made in Denmark; also comes caraway seeded.

VACHERIN FONDUE: Made in Switzerland much the same as Swiss. After it is cured, it is melted and spices added.

VERMONT MAPLE and VERMONT SAGE: Cheddar cheeses made in that state with the addition of maple flavoring or sage herb.

WARWICKSHIRE: An English cheese very similar to Derby.

WENSLEYDALE: Creamy Yorkshire cheese with subtle flavor, flaky texture and pale parchment color.

WILTSHIRE: Another English cheese similar to Derby; Cheddar family.

WISCONSIN TOP HAT: An American Cheddar, usually aged and sharp.

The apricot-yellow color of the Cheddars, Cheshires and American cheese is not natural, but due to the addition of annatto, a harmless vegetable dye.

Before it was discovered, 200 years ago, all sorts of other dyes were tried, some toxic and others adding an undesirable taste. The leaves of wild pot marigold, carrot juice, saffron and even common household dyes were tried.

And in those bad old days, unscrupulous grocers bored holes in ordinary pale cheese and sold it as "Swiss"!

SOME OFF-BEAT SEASONINGS TO ADD TO CHEESE FONDUES

Caraway seeds and fresh caraway
Celery seed and salt
Crumbled crisp bacon
Crumbled basil leaves
Minced green and red (sweet) pepper
½ teaspoon oregano
½ teaspoon marjoram
A.1. Sauce
Minced stuffed green olives
Bahamian mustard

Curry powder
Chili powder
H.P. Sauce
Chervil
Sesame seed
Mustard seed
Saffron
Peppermint
Rosemary
Sage
Thyme
Dill, fresh and seed

That delightful dancer Marge (Mrs. Gower) Champion serves a delicious fondue which features ice-cold vegetables dipped in very hot cheese fondue. You can emulate her and have a hit party by using your favorite among the fondues presented above and, instead of dipping cubes of French bread therein, using any or all of the following vegetables.

1 small head raw cauliflower, broken into flowerets
12 young carrots, scraped and cut into strips
4 cucumbers, peeled, seeded and in strips or half-strips
4 zucchini, cut lengthwise in quarters

2 small summer squash, in quarters
1 bunch celery hearts, separated
1 bunch long white radishes, trimmed and in quarters, lengthwise
1 bunch small red radishes, with stems on

12 scallions, trimmed

Arrange all the vegetables as artistically as you can on a tray or platter and chill in refrigerator for at least an hour before serving time.

FONDUES IN PACKAGES

For people in a hurry or hesitant about trying out their fondue sets for the first time—or just plain lazy—there are a number of prepared fondues which have been imported in cans or packages. Apparently U.S. food packagers have not yet discovered the fondue as a convenience food. These ready-to-use fondues are from Switzerland mostly, contain all the ingredients, are popped right into the pot, and are for 4 people. Depending on where you purchase them, they retail at from one to three dollars, with most around two dollars. They are listed here in alphabetical order.

BLITZ, Original Schweitzer Fondue "Cow Brand," Cheese Export, Ltd. Emmental, Switzerland. Genuine Swiss Emmentaler and Gruyère cheese, starch, emulsifying salts, Swiss wine, kirsch and spices. Ready in about 6 minutes. 14 ounces, 2–3 persons.

CHALET Cheese Fondue, in aluminum bags and cans, Chalet Cheese Co. Ltd., Burgdorf, Switzerland. Swiss and natural Gruyère, white Swiss wine, white cherry brandy (kirsch), paprika, garlic, nutmeg, etc. Prepared in 5 minutes. 14 ounces. Keep in cool place.

Fondue Variations:

Ham and Fondue: There is no reason why you can't substitute cubes of ham for traditional French bread.

Egg Fondue: When there is only a third or so fondue left in your pot or chafing dish, drop in one or two raw eggs. Mix slowly with a fork while the fondue cooks over the small flame.

Hot Cheese Dip: For an unusual party dip, surround your chafing dish with chips and assorted crackers. Greedy scoopers break chips, so warn your guests to dip only.

Fondue on Toast: Use regular white toast for this

"hot cheese sandwich." Not traditional, but luscious and delightful just the same.

LA VRAIE Fondue, Gresse, France. In cans, keep refrigerated but not in deep freeze. Add glass very dry wine. Ready in 5 minutes. 14¾ ounces, 4 portions.

SWISS KNIGHT Fondue, in bags, Gerber Cheese Co. Ltd., Thoune, Switzerland. Original Gruyère and Emmentaler cheese, white wine and kirsch. 14 ounces, do not keep in deep freeze.

Flavor Variations:

Spicy Fondue: Rub the inside of the chafing dish with a cut clove of garlic and add a dash of nutmeg. Or add a few drops of Tabasco for real zest.

Curried Fondue: Stir in ½ to 1 teaspoon curry powder.

Fondue Diable: Add ½ teaspoon mustard.

Tomato Fondue: Add catsup to taste—about 1 tablespoon.

Onion Fondue Dip: Add ¼ cup heavy cream and 2 tablespoons dehydrated onion soup mix. Reheat and serve.

SWISSALP Fondue, made in Switzerland. Swiss cheese and Gruyère, flavored with Swiss wine, kirsch and spices. 14 ounces, 2–3 persons.

SWISSETTE Fondue, in bags, Emmental Co. Ltd., Zollenkofen, Switzerland. Swiss Emmentaler and Gruyère cheese, white wine, cornstarch, sodium phosphate and kirsch. Ready to serve. 14 ounces, 2 portions.

TIGER SWISS FONDUE, in package, Roethlisberger and Son, Ltd., Langnau/Emmental, Switzerland. Emmentaler and Gruyère cheese, white wine, kirsch, cornstarch, sodium phosphate. (Information came from Sicily, where it is sold.)

VERITABLE CANCOILLOTTE DE FRANCHE-COMTÉ, in cans, refrigerate but do not freeze. H. Julien, Champigny-sur-Marne, France. Soft ripened pasteurized cheese with butter. In 15-ounce and 7-ounce cans.

ZINGG Fondue, in envelopes, Zingg Co., Berne, Switzerland. Swiss Emmentaler cheese, Gruyère cheese, white wine, kirsch, cornstarch. 14 ounces, refrigerate but do not freeze.

ZINGG Swiss Fondue, in cans, Zingg Co., Berne, Switzerland. Cheese, water, wine, kirsch, cornstarch, sodium citrate. 15 ounces, for 2–3 people.

Instructions on the napkins at The Wine and Cheese, Chelsea, London:

SWISS CHEESE FONDUE

"Spear a small piece of bread with your Fondue Fork and dip it into the Fondue, stir round the pot once or twice, and then pop this delicious morsel into your mouth.

"A most important Fondue rule is: he who loses a piece of bread in the mixture has to pay for a bottle of wine or for the next Fondue. Only ladies are free of this venerable law; they forfeit a kiss for every piece of bread they lose."

Which brings up the question for us practical Americans: Which man should the girl kiss, the one on the right or the man on her other side? If she has leftish tendencies there is no question. If she's the non-partisan type, she can kiss both of them. In case this is too tame —or she's lost a number of pieces, she should take one of the men into the other room and explain the Women's Liberation Movement—with gestures.

Seafood and Fish Fondues

Konrad Egli, whose Chalet Suisse on 48th Street, off Fifth Avenue in N.Y.C. is a focal point for fondue fanciers, is the creator of Fondue aux Fruits de Mer, or

DEEP SEA FONDUE A LA CHALET SUISSE
[Serves 4 to 6]

Fish Bouillon

4 cups bottled clam juice	1 large carrot, minced
2 cups dry white wine	1 stalk celery, fine-chopped
2 cups water	4 peppercorns
1 large onion, minced	1 bay leaf

½ teaspoon salt

In saucepan, bring liquids to a boil, then simmer all ingredients over moderate heat 30 minutes.

Strain and use liquid in fondue pot, discarding solids.

Seafoods for Dunking

1 pound filets of sole, cut in strips 2 inches long	12 large sea scallops, each in 3 slices

4 lobster tails, cut in bite-sized pieces

Method: At serving time, heat bouillon in fondue pot and keep at simmer point at table over burner.

Provide each guest with one-fourth of the seafoods (or ⅙) on an individual plate, plus a wooden fork for dunking and eating (or two metal forks, one for cooking—which will get very hot—and one for eating).

Each guest cooks his own seafood, a piece at a time, in the simmering bouillon: 30–45 seconds for sole, about 1 minute each for scallop slices and 1½ minutes for the lobster chunks. Only long enough for the flesh to turn white.

(Bay scallops, smaller and more tender than the sea scallops, require less cooking.)

Provide each guest further with lemon wedges and a variety of sauces (see below).

When all of the seafood has been cooked and eaten, divide the wonderful, concentrated bouillon into bowls and have this delicious sup at the end of the meal!

TARTAR SAUCE
[Makes 1½ cups]

4 scallions, white part only,
  fine-chopped
1 small sour pickle, minced
¼ cup pimiento-stuffed green
  olives, minced

1 cup mayonnaise
2 tablespoons parsley,
  fine-chopped
Salt and white pepper

Combine scallions, pickle and olives; blend thoroughly with mayonnaise. Stir in parsley. Season to taste with salt and white pepper.

LOBSTER SAUCE
[Makes about 1¼ cups]

2 cups water
  Shells from lobster tails
2 tablespoons butter
2 tablespoons flour
2 tablespoons whipped cream

2 teaspoons Hollandaise
  Sauce without cucumber
  (see below)
Salt and white pepper to
  taste

Boil shells in water 20 minutes, until resulting stock is reduced to about half. Strain and discard shells. Bring stock back to boil and hold it there.

In separate saucepan melt butter over low heat. Do not brown. Add flour and stir into a well-blended roux.

Still stirring roux, add boiling stock all at once. Beat briskly to blend in. Turn heat up to moderate, bring sauce to boil and, while stirring, allow to boil 1 minute.

Turn heat down to simmer and stir in whipped cream and Hollandaise. Blend. Season with salt and pepper and remove from heat. Chill before serving.

HOLLANDAISE-CUCUMBER SAUCE
[Makes over 1 cup]

3 egg yolks	1½ sticks unsalted butter
1 tablespoon lemon juice	2 tablespoons cucumber,
¼ teaspoon salt	peeled, seeded, grated

In top of double boiler combine egg yolks, lemon juice and salt. Set pan over simmering water. Immediately add 4 tablespoons (½ stick) butter; beat mixture until butter is completely incorporated. Add another 4 tablespoons butter and beat in. Repeat with remaining 4 tablespoons butter. When completely incorporated, sauce will have thickened sufficiently. Do not overcook.

Remove pan from water; let sauce cool slightly.

Two teaspoons of the Hollandaise may be reserved for Lobster Sauce (above).

Using cheesecloth, press out all liquid from the cucumber. Blend dried, grated cucumber into sauce; serve at once.

Note: If salted butter is used, omit the salt in recipe.

SKIPPER'S FONDUE

6 to 8 ounces per person of	slices of fish from sea
shrimp/crayfish/lobster/	Batter (optional)
Cooking oil	

Have lobster in bite-size pieces. Cut fish in not-too-thin slices and roll and fasten with skewers.

Guests can either dip seafood and fish in batter, then in sizzling oil, or plunge in oil unadorned.

Tartar Sauce, Mustard Sauces, Mayonnaise, Hollandaise Sauce and Tomato Sauces are among those that go well; plus crisp rolls and a green salad. The Spring Fondue equipment people of Switzerland also recommend "a prickling white wine or a fresh beer."

Here are 4 sauces that are especially delicious with a Skipper's Fondue.

AURORE SAUCE
[Makes ½ cup]

½ cup mayonnaise
1 tablespoon tomato catsup

½ teaspoon Worcestershire sauce
1 teaspoon brandy

Combine ingredients in order given and blend well. Also excellent for shrimp cocktail.

VINAIGRETTE SAUCE
[Makes over 1 cup]

½ cup olive or salad oil
1 large hard-cooked egg, chopped fine
3 tablespoons tarragon vinegar
1 tablespoon minced parsley
1 tablespoon minced green pepper
1 tablespoon chopped sweet

pepper
2 teaspoons capers
2 teaspoons minced chives
1 teaspoon salt
¼ teaspoon paprika
⅛ teaspoon fresh-ground pepper
Dash onion juice (optional)
Dash cayenne

Blend well together and chill in refrigerator.

QUICK VINAIGRETTE
[Makes 1 cup]

¾ cup French dressing
1 hard-cooked egg,

fine-chopped
1 teaspoon minced chives

Mix thoroughly and chill.

SAUCE TARTARE
[Makes 1 cup]

1 hard-cooked egg yolk
3 small sweet pickles
4 shallots

1 tablespoon capers
1 small bunch parsley
5 tablespoons mayonnaise

Chop egg yolk, pickles, shallots, capers and parsley fine. Mix thoroughly with the mayonnaise and chill.

LOBSTER FONDUE
[Serves 12 as appetizer or 4 as main fondue]

1 can frozen condensed
    cream of shrimp soup,
    thawed
½ soup can milk
½ cup shredded mellow
    Cheddar cheese

4 ounces (½ cup) cooked or
    canned lobster, diced
Dash paprika
Dash cayenne
2 tablespoons sherry

Combine soup and milk in fondue pot over low heat and stir occasionally until mixture approaches boil. Add cheese, lobster, paprika and cayenne. Heat again, stirring often until cheese melts. Add sherry.

Use as appetizer dunk with squares of crusty French bread or as main dish for a meal.

Can also be poured over toast slices spread with dill butter as luncheon dish.

As I was approaching the deadline for this book, I received a long-distance call from Palm Springs, California. It was Eleanor Barnes Mare who wanted to be sure I received her shrimp fondue recipe, which she proceeded to dictate over the telephone. Here it is:

MRS. MARE'S SHRIMP FONDUE
[Serves 4 to 6]

2 pounds peeled raw shrimp
1 cup safflower seed oil

12 cooked artichoke hearts in
    bite-sized pieces
Super Sauce (see below)

Fill a 2½-quart saucepan half full of water and bring to a rolling boil. Cook shrimp 5 minutes.

Drain in colander, devein and rinse.

Put oil in fondue pot and heat to sizzling. Bring to table and keep hot over Sterno or other heat.

Each guest pierces shrimp or artichoke bit on fondue fork and cooks it until it is done the way he likes it. Then he dips it into the Super Sauce.

SUPER SAUCE
[Makes 2½ cups]

1 cup mayonnaise	1 teaspoon onion flakes
1 cup sour cream	1 teaspoon parsley flakes
2 teaspoons curry powder	1 teaspoon coarse salt
1 teaspoon chopped capers	½ teaspoon Lawry's
1 teaspoon dry mustard	Marinade (optional)

1 jigger good brandy

Stir together all ingredients except brandy and let stand 20 minutes. Add brandy and stir again.

PINEAPPLE FONDUE

An hors d'oeuvre fondue. Consists of 1 can of pineapple chunks, drained, on skewers or toothpicks, to be dipped into the above Super Sauce.

QUICK SHRIMP FONDUE
[Serves 4]

1 can frozen shrimp soup, thawed	2 tablespoons dry white wine
1 cup shredded Gruyère cheese	Cubes of pumpernickel, rye or French bread

In fondue pot over medium heat, heat soup. Add cheese and stir often until melted. Stir in wine and when hot dip in chunks of bread on wooden forks.

BAY SCALLOP FONDUE
[Serves 4 to 6]

2 pounds little bay scallops   1 pint chicken consommé
1 pint clam juice   ½ cup dry white wine

Divide scallops among plates of guests. (Cut-up ocean scallops can be used, but you won't get the delicate flavor and texture.)

In fondue pot or casserole, bring clam juice, consommé and wine to a boil. Place on table over warmer.

Each guest spears scallop on fondue fork and cooks in pot until it is just done. Remove and dip in one of sauces below.

AVOCADO SAUCE
[Makes about 1 cup]

1 ripe avocado, peeled and   Juice of ½ lemon
    mashed   1 clove garlic, crushed
3 tablespoons mayonnaise   (optional)

Blend thoroughly. Serve chilled.

RED SEA SAUCE
[Makes ⅔ cup]

8 tablespoons plain yogurt or   2 teaspoons prepared
    sour cream   horseradish
2 tablespoons catsup or chili   3 drops Tabasco sauce
    sauce

Blend and mix well. Chill before serving.

CUT-A-CAPER SAUCE
[Makes 1¼ cups]

1 cup mayonnaise   1 teaspoon chopped parsley
4 tablespoons chopped capers   1 teaspoon dry mustard
              1 teaspoon lemon juice

Blend all ingredients thoroughly and chill before serving.

CAPRI SAUCE
[Makes 1¼ cups]

½ cup sour cream
½ cup mayonnaise
2 tablespoons chopped
   pickle
1 tablespoon minced onion

1 tablespoon chopped
   parsley
1 tablespoon chopped green
   olives
1 teaspoon white vinegar
¼ teaspoon Tabasco sauce

Combine and mix well. Keep in refrigerator until ready to serve.

Mrs. James J. Kilian who lives on the Palos Verdes Peninsula in California is a very pretty girl named Joe Ann. Naturally her fondue recipe has the flavor of the sea. It is also very quickly made and practical for when unexpected parties drop in for unexpected parties.

JOE ANN'S FAST EMERGENCY FONDUE
[Serves 4]

2 cans minced clams
3 jars Old English Cheese
½ green pepper, chopped fine
1 bunch fresh green onions,

chopped fine
1 teaspoon Worcestershire
   sauce
Dash garlic powder

Drain liquid from clams, reserving ¼ cup.

Mix the minced clams with other ingredients. Put in saucepan and melt over low heat, adding the reserved clam liquid.

Serve hot in fondue pot with crinkle potato chips.

Note: This fondue can be stored in freezer in small plastic containers for emergency occasions.

In the autumn, as soon as the mussels come into season in London, Walter Baxter of the Chanterelle in Chelsea begins to serve the following:

CHANTERELLE MUSSEL FONDUE
[Serves 8]

9 tablespoons butter	2 cups cubed Gruyère
5 tablespoons flour	cheese
1¼ pints boiling milk	4 dozen mussels
2 egg yolks	½ cup dry white wine
	½ cup water

Cook 5 tablespoons of the butter and the flour together in saucepan for 3 to 5 minutes; do not allow to color. Reduce heat and beat boiling milk in slowly.

Remove from heat and beat in egg yolks vigorously. Add cheese and stir until melted. Then add remaining 4 tablespoons of butter. Season with salt, pepper and nutmeg to taste.

Wash, scrub mussels and poach in wine and water until shells open; remove beards. Allow ½ dozen mussels and ½ cup cheese sauce for each person and reheat in ramekins in oven.

FRENCH FRIED HALIBUT (Flétans à l'Orly)
[Serves 4]

2½ pounds halibut	Olive oil for deep frying
Salt	Green Sauce (see below)

Batter

1 cup sifted flour	Salt to taste
1 egg	1 teaspoon oil
	1 cup beer

Skin and bone halibut and cut into cubes. Sprinkle with salt.

Prepare batter by combining flour, egg, salt, oil and beer and mixing well.

Each guest is served with cubes of fish and skewers. He dips each cube in batter, then into olive oil bubbling in fondue pot until it is quickly cooked, then takes it out and dips it into Green Sauce, served in individual bowls.

GREEN SAUCE

1 pint mayonnaise
1½ tablespoons chopped
 chervil
1½ tablespoons chopped
 chives

1½ tablespoons chopped
 parsley
1½ tablespoons lemon juice

Blend herbs into mayonnaise until well integrated. Flavor with lemon juice.

In response to my query for fondue recipes made to a couple who are among my oldest friends, the Maxwell Shanes collaborated on this recipe—that is, Evelyn dictated and Max typed.

"When I was a bride, I had very few dishes or pots, but I had two chafing dishes which had been given us as wedding presents. So I learned how to cook in those before I learned anything else in the culinary department. Following is a simple chafing dish recipe which I used to make whenever we had guests. And from the lip-smacking it engendered, it must have been very popular."

TUNA FONDUE EVELYN
[Serves 4]

½ pound sharp Cheddar
 cheese
Half-and-half
1 7-ounce can flaked tuna

2 ounces Chablis or Sauterne
 Paprika
Toasted French bread, in
 cubes

Crumble the cheese into chafing dish blazer pan over direct heat, adding enough half-and-half to give the cheese a loose paste consistency. Add the tuna, stirring constantly to keep it from lumping. When the mixture is smooth and bubbling nicely, add the wine, continuing to stir until well-blended again.

When ready, sprinkle with enough paprika to give it color. Do not stir after adding paprika. Dip toasted French bread.

Variation: Practically the same result can be obtained by using a can of Cheddar soup instead of the cheese and half-and-half.

"P.S. I used to eat this stuff until my tongue clung to the roof of my mouth, but it was good. Now we seldom have guests at home, going out for dinner most of the time, and suffering the less tasteful restaurant food."
—Max.

SOME MORE SEAFOOD DIPS

ANCHOVY CATSUP
[Makes 2 cups]

1 quart ale	mushrooms
¼ pound anchovies	½ teaspoon sugar
3 shallots, fine-chopped	½ teaspoon ground ginger
3 tablespoons catsup	¼ teaspoon ground mace
1 tablespoon broiled, minced	2 cloves

Simmer all ingredients together, very gently, for 1 hour. Strain. Use cold.

SPUN SOUR CREAM SAUCE
[Makes 1½ cups]

1 cup sour cream	½ teaspoon Worcestershire
2 egg yolks	sauce
1 tablespoon lemon juice	¼ teaspoon curry powder
½ teaspoon dry mustard	¼ teaspoon salt

Place ingredients in blender and mix thoroughly. Pour into saucepan and heat over low heat until sauce thickens.

COCKTAIL SAUCE
[Makes almost 1 pint]

1 cup tomato catsup
5 tablespoons chili sauce
4 tablespoons lemon juice
4 tablespoons prepared

horseradish (or 1½
  tablespoons grated)
½ teaspoon celery salt
8 drops Tabasco sauce

Combine ingredients and blend well. Chill.

SEAFOOD SAUCE
[Over 1 cup]

9 tablespoons chili sauce
3 tablespoons lemon juice
3 tablespoons mayonnaise
1 tablespoon prepared horse-

radish
1 tablespoon prepared mustard
3 drops Tabasco sauce

Blend well and chill.

Broth Fondues

To preface this group of Oriental fondue dishes, I recall the only two eating rules the Chinese have:
1. No unpleasant conversation.
2. No table manners.

MONGOLIAN BEEF HOT POT
[Serves 4]

2 pounds flank steak

Marinade

½ cup soy sauce
½ cup Chinese rice wine or
    dry sherry
¼ teaspoon sesame oil

1 clove garlic, minced
⅛ teaspoon baking soda
2 tablespoons cornstarch
¼ cup salad oil

Broth

½ cup soy sauce
½ cup chicken broth
4 teaspoons white wine
    vinegar
4 teaspoons sherry

1 teaspoon salt
½ teaspoon sugar
1 large bunch green onions
¼ cup salad or cooking oil
Hot cooked rice

Cut steak across the grain into slices about ⅙-inch thick.

Marinade: Combine soy sauce, wine, sesame oil, garlic, soda.

Mix cornstarch with a little of the above liquid, then mix the paste into the marinade. Add the salad oil, blend well. Soak beef slices in marinade in refrigerator 2 hours.

While marinating beef, combine other soy sauce, broth, vinegar, sherry, salt, and sugar and mix well.

Trim green onions and use only white part; slice diagonally into 2-inch lengths.

Heat metal fondue pot over high heat with additional ¼ cup oil. Add beef and its marinade and, stirring well, brown very lightly. Add onions and stir-fry 1 minute. Add broth mixture and stir and cook 1 minute. Serve with rice.

The two following recipes were originally intended to be cooked in a Mongolian Hot Pot, which uses charcoal in a chimney in the center of the cooker, surrounded by a ring for the broth which is heated to bubbling and in which the meat is cooked. However, because the fumes from burning charcoal are dangerous, these pots are not recommended. Jack Loo of Ying's Restaurant on lower Fifth Avenue where these Mandarin dishes are served during the winter tells me that Mongolian Hot Pots are prohibited by law in New York City.

MIXED MANDARIN HOT POT
[Serves 4 or 5]

Breasts from 1 medium chicken
½ pound beefsteak
12 large shrimp
½ head Chinese cabbage (or 1 head lettuce)
1½ cups halved fresh Chinese (black) mushrooms
1 5-ounce can water chest-nuts (or 1 cup cubed eggplant)
4 cups torn fresh spinach leaves, stems removed
2 tall (13¾-ounce) cans chicken broth
1 teaspoon grated fresh ginger (or ¼ teaspoon ground ginger)

Skin, bone and slice the two chicken breasts across the grain. Slice beefsteak in thin slices across grain. Peel, devein and clean shrimp. Cube Chinese cabbage or trimmed head of lettuce coarsely. Slice water chestnuts very thin. Arrange all but spinach on platter, cover with aluminum foil or plastic wrap and refrigerate until an hour or so before serving. Then bring to room temperature. Tear spinach and place in a serving bowl.

When guests are at table, pour chicken broth and

ginger into fondue pot and heat to gentle boil. Regulate flame to keep broth that way. Add more broth if needed.

Using chopsticks, fondue forks, skewers or wooden tongs, guests hold meat, shrimp or vegetables in broth until cooked to their liking, then lift out and dip in sauces (Hot Mustard, Soy, etc.). Serve hot, fluffy rice on side.

Bonus: When all the food has been eaten, raw eggs may be poached in the broth, 1 to a customer.

Bonus No. 2: After the eggs are eaten (or they may be skipped) add ¼ cup Chinese rice wine or dry sherry to broth and serve in Chinese tea cups.

LAMB FIRE POT
[Serves 6]

¼ pound cellophane noodles[1]   der lamb (boneless)
3 pounds lean leg or shoul-   ½ pound fresh spinach
½ pound Chinese cabbage

Sauce

2 tablespoons plain peanut butter
1 tablespoon brown sugar
Boiling water
½ cup soy sauce
2 tablespoons Chinese rice wine (or dry sherry)
2 tablespoons sesame oil
1 tablespoon fermented bean curd (optional)
¼ teaspoon cayenne

8 cups fresh or canned chicken stock or con-sommé
2 green onions, minced
1 tablespoon fine-chopped, peeled fresh ginger root or 1 teaspoon ground ginger
¼ cup minced Chinese or flat-leaf parsley
1 teaspoon minced garlic

Soak cellophane noodles overnight in salted water, or boil 10 minutes. Drain and place on platter.

Have butcher cut lamb against grain in thinnest possible slices, or chill 2 hours to firm for easy slicing and do same yourself. Cut slices into small rectangles, 2 × 3 inches, and divide into 6 portions on individual plates.

Trim stems and stalks from spinach, wash under cold

---

[1] Cellophane noodles can be bought in Chinese groceries.

running water; drain and dry well. Place on platter with noodles.

Trim outside leaves and root of cabbage; separate into stalks and wash under cold running water. Cut into 1 × 3-inch pieces. In pot of boiling water, drop pieces for 3 minutes; drain, dry well and place on platter with spinach and noodles.

Make sauce by combining in large bowl the peanut butter and sugar with 3 tablespoons boiling water, blending well; add the soy sauce, wine, oil, bean curd and cayenne, blending well again. Prepare 6 small servings and serve remainder in community bowl.

In fondue pot heat chicken stock to boil; keep simmering or bubbling during meal. Add more broth if needed.

Give each guest plate of meat and the sauce. Have other ingredients handy.

Drop green onions, ginger, parsley and garlic into pot.

Give guests fondue forks with which they will cook their own lamb to desired doneness.

When finished with meat, drop noodles, spinach and cabbage into pot, cook for 1 minute and serve with broth as vegetable soup.

Marcia Hale, a past president of the Federation of American Women's Clubs Overseas and a resident of Zurich, sent me this non-fattening

FONDUE CHINOISE
[Serves 4]

2 pounds beef filet	3 cups chicken broth
	Dash sherry

Relish Tray

Raw carrot sticks	Pickles
Scallions	Olives
Cauliflowerets	Horseradish sauce
Cucumber strips	French bread, spread with
Radishes	garlic butter
Thousand Island Dressing	

Have butcher freeze beef and slice it very thin on his slicing machine. Fasten with skewers in bite-sized rolls.

Fill fondue pot with chicken broth made fresh or with cubes or canned. If either of latter two, do not salt. Add sherry and keep bubbling over medium-hot heat.

Fill large sectioned platter with relish tray vegetables. Put Sauce and Dressing in two bowls, or individual small dishes for each diner.

Serve rolled meat on individual plates decorated with parsley. Meat is held in chicken broth for long enough to cook it the way each guest prefers.

"The splendid part of Fondue Chinoise is the rich chicken broth you wind up with, served at the end of the meal," writes Marcia. "This Fondue dinner can be prepared in advance—even the day before. It is decorative, nourishing and POW!"

A wide variety of red and white wine can be served with this meal, such as a Beaujolais, Bordeaux, Dole, Fendant, Pinot Noir of Valais, Neuchâtel, Grisons and Merlot from Ticino, the reds at room temperature.

When I sent out a call all over the world for recipes for this fondue cook book, one of the first responses was from Rosemary Cartwright in Washington who sent me a number of valuable recipes, including

FONDUE ORIENTALE
[Serves 4]

½ pound lean beef
½ pound thin-sliced lean veal
½ pound lean pork
6 lamb kidneys (cores re-
moved)
6 cups chicken stock, broth, consommé or bouillon
Salt and pepper to taste

Slice all meat wafer-thin and bite-size. Serve on individual plates.

Heat broth to boiling and pour into fondue pot over sufficient heat to keep it at a brisk simmer.

Guests spear meat on forks from off their plates and cook to desired state in the hot broth.

When meat is all gone, enriched broth is divided into

individual cups and drunk by diners. Or broth can be added to hot fluffy rice, which is then apportioned among diners.

Among the sauces recommended with Fondue Orientale are Béarnaise, A.1., Escoffier Robert, Horseradish, plus mustard and catsup.

BEEF FONDUE ORIENTALE

7 ounces tender beef per person

5 to 6 cups bouillon (beef or chicken)

Slice meat into very thin slices about 4 inches long, and roll up. It is easier to slice if meat is partly frozen.

Instead of using oil as in Fondue Bourguignon, Fondue Orientale uses bouillon. Fill the pot about 2/3 full with bouillon, and heat to just under boiling.

Spear the meat and dip into hot bouillon to cook. Do not salt the meat or you will destroy your after-dinner broth. After dipping and cooking the meat, dip into any of the sauces given for Fondue Bourguignon (See Index). Use 4 or 5 sauces.

When everyone is done cooking in the broth, add ½ cup sherry, and serve in cups.

ELECTRIC FONDUE ORIENTALE
[Serves 4]

2 pounds chicken breast, beef or pork tenderloin, lamb

or veal or mixture
3 cups chicken or beef broth

Cut meat into paper-thin strips. Do not season, or broth will become too salty.

Put broth into electric fondue pot and heat to boiling at highest heat; reduce to medium to keep broth at a rolling boil while cooking meat.

Roll bite-sized portions of meat and pierce with skewer or wooden fork and cook in broth until done the way each guest likes it. Be sure to cook pork thoroughly.

Serve plain or seasoned rice with above; and cucumber

or green salad or green vegetable, plus fresh fruit and fortune cookies.

Note: After meat is finished, lace remaining broth with sherry or white wine and serve in demitasse cups.

FONDUE COQ AU VIN
[Serves 4]

2 cups Burgundy wine
2 cups chicken consommé
½ teaspoon salt
¼ teaspoon fresh-crushed pepper
1 tablespoon fine-chopped fresh or 1 teaspoon dried tarragon

¼ cup fine-chopped scallions, including green part
1½ pounds sliced white meat chicken in 1-inch squares
3 ounces brandy

In saucepan, simmer wine, consommé, salt, pepper, tarragon and scallions 15 minutes. Pour into fondue pot and bring to table over heat that will keep liquid simmering.

Spear squares of chicken on skewers or fondue forks and cook in hot broth-wine until done to taste. Remove, take off metal forks to avoid burning mouth, and dip into assortment of creamy sauces.

When all meat has been cooked, add brandy to liquid in pot, then strain into individual cups for guests to finish meal on a liquid note.

The French
Melting Vegetable Fondues

Here are a dozen recipes for a different kind of fondue—
just about a puree of vegetable, used in other dishes and
as a side dish to accompany meat or fish.

FONDUE OF CARROTS

In a closed saucepan, stew 1 pound of thinly-sliced
carrots with butter, seasoned with salt and a soupçon of
sugar.

To prevent the carrots from frying in the butter add,
now and then, a little water or broth. Cook until the
carrots are completely melted.

FONDUE OF CELERY

Cut up stalks of celery or celery root. Melt some
butter with 1 pound thinly-sliced celery. Season with
salt and pepper and add a little water or broth to prevent the celery from frying. Cook until the water or
broth is completely evaporated.

FONDUE OF TUBEROSE CHERVIL

In France, a tuberous-rooted variety of chervil is grown
and eaten like carrots. The fondue is prepared in the
same manner as the Fondue of Celery, above.

FONDUE OF ENDIVE (broad-leaf chicory)

Slice thin one pound raw chicory and stew gently with butter in covered pan. Season with salt and pepper. Used to decorate egg dishes, fish, fowl or small servings of meat.

FONDUE OF TUBEROSE FENNEL

The blanched stems and bulbous bases of sweet fennel are eaten raw, like celery, and made into a fondue in the same manner as celery.

FONDUE OF LEEKS

Sliced thin, the white of leeks is melted with butter like other vegetables and seasoned similarly. It is used as a sauce or stuffing or with meat or fowl.

FONDUE OF LETTUCE

Trim ½ pound lettuce of thick ribs, shred and place in pan with 2 tablespoons butter. Season to taste with salt and pepper and cook gently until all water has evaporated, stirring occasionally with wooden spoon.

You may add 3 spoonfuls of fresh cream at the beginning of cooking.

Used with boiled eggs, sirloin, or poultry.

FONDUE OF MUSHROOMS

Use thin-sliced mushrooms, mix with cream and breadcrumbs and brown in the oven.

FONDUE OF ONIONS

Stew 1 pound thin-sliced or chopped onions in covered pot with butter, but do not let them brown, adding either water or broth in small quantities. Season with salt and pepper and "melt."

FONDUE OF PIMIENTOS

Slice 1 pound pimiento peppers very thin and melt them gently in butter or oil by same method described above.

Use as stuffing or as a sauce with eggs, fish, shellfish, meat, fowl or with vegetables.

FONDUE OF TOMATOES

Peel and trim 6 small tomatoes and cut up into dice.

Cook gently in butter or ½ butter and ½ olive oil 4 ounces of thin-chopped onions until they begin to brown. Add the tomatoes, season with salt and pepper and a bit of garlic juice.

Simmer until all the water has evaporated from tomatoes. At last minute, stir in ½ teaspoon of chopped parsley.

These are called Tomatoes à la Provençale, or Tomatoes à la Madrilène, or à la Portugaise. Particularly useful for stuffing zucchini and other squash, eggplant and artichoke bottoms.

FONDUE OF TOMATOES A LA NICOISE

Proceed as above but at finish, add tarragon, instead of parsley, and a touch of saffron.

A DIFFERENT TOMATO FONDUE
A LA NICOISE
[Serves 4]

1 tablespoon olive oil	Salt and pepper
1 tablespoon butter	1 clove garlic, crushed
1 medium onion, sliced	(optional)
6 medium tomatoes, peeled, seeded, chopped	1 teaspoon oregano

Heat oil and melt butter in skillet or saucepan, add onion and sauté until tender. Add tomatoes, season to taste and add garlic. Simmer over low heat until liquid has evaporated and tomatoes have thick, smooth consistency, about 15 minutes. Sprinkle with oregano.

One teaspoon chopped fresh chervil (¼ teaspoon dried) or 1 tablespoon chopped fresh tarragon (1 teaspoon dried) may be substituted for oregano.

Excellent served as a side dish with broiled fish. To serve with baked fish, add to baking pan as garnish when fish is half-cooked.

VEGETABLE FONDUE

2 carrots in thin slices	Salt to taste
1 turnip in thin slices	1 teaspoon sugar
White of 1 leek	1 tablespoon butter
¼ celery knob in thin slices	¼ pint veal broth

Mix vegetables in saucepan, season with salt and sugar. Cook in pan with butter. When vegetables have melted and are mahogany in color, add veal broth and let it boil down gently until all of the broth has evaporated.

Used with eggs and fish.

Baked Fondues

Another type of dish called "fondue" is a baked pudding which probably gets its name because it contains cheese which is melted in the process of baking.

Even the Rombauers' *Joy of Cooking* defines Fondue as "A baked dish not unlike a soufflé usually including bread or cracker crumbs."

The first one can be made in the morning for use as a main dish at dinner, or at night, for baking the following day.

WESTERN BAKED FONDUE
[Serves 6]

12 slices bread of your choice
6 tablespoons soft butter or margarine
1 12-ounce can whole kernel corn (or corn and peppers), drained
1 7-ounce can green chili peppers
2 cups shredded Monterey Jack cheese
4 eggs, slightly beaten
3 cups milk
1 teaspoon salt

Trim crusts from bread and spread with butter. Cut each slice in half.

Butter shallow 3-quart baking dish and arrange half the bread on bottom. Cover with half the corn.

Seed and stem the chili peppers and cut into strips. Decorate corn layer with half the strips. Cover with half the cheese. Repeat layers of bread, corn, chili strips and cheese.

Mix together the eggs, milk and salt and pour over casserole ingredients.

Cover and refrigerate at least 4 hours.

Uncover and bake at 350° until puffy and brown, 45 to 50 minutes.

This recipe was brought to my attention by Deaconess Maude Behrman, one of America's best-regarded dietitians and formerly head of the Lankenau School of Nursing, dietetics department, where this was popular with the students.

BAKED CHEESE FONDUE
[Serves 4 to 6]

1 cup shredded Cheddar cheese	1 tablespoon butter or margarine
1 cup hot milk	⅛ teaspoon salt
1 cup soft breadcrumbs	3 eggs, separated

Blend cheese, milk, breadcrumbs, butter and salt. Beat egg yolks well; stir in a little of milk mixture, then stir rest of yolks into hot milk mixture.

Beat egg whites until they hold stiff peaks, then fold into mixture, gently.

Pour into buttered 1- or 1½-quart baking dish and bake in preheated 350° oven for 25 to 30 minutes, until toothpick inserted in center comes out clean.

Serve immediately.

ANOTHER SAVOIE FONDUE
[Serves 4 to 6]

6 eggs	3 tablespoons cream
2 cups Gruyère or Beaufort or Comté cheese, in small dice	½ teaspoon fresh-crushed pepper
	4 tablespoons butter, in bits
1 cup dry white wine	

Beat eggs in bowl; add cheese, cream, pepper, butter and wine; blend well. Pour into earthenware casserole, or coquelin, with handle and bake in preheated 350° oven for 30 minutes.

Remove carefully to fondue stand over medium heat and proceed as with other cheese fondues.

Chicken à la King, originally called Chicken à la Keene, after the man who introduced it to Delmonico's, is the garnish for this baked fondue.

BAKED FONDUE WITH CHICKEN A LA KING
[Serves 8 to 12]

Fondue

2 cups stale soft bread-crumbs	2 tablespoons butter
	1 teaspoon salt
½ pound sharp Cheddar cheese, grated	2 cups scalded milk
	6 eggs, separated

Mix breadcrumbs, grated cheese, butter and salt. Add hot milk and blend well. Beat egg yolks well and add to mixture. Whip egg whites to peaks and cut and fold into mixture.

Pour into buttered square baking dish and bake in 350° oven 20 minutes.

Chicken à la King

2 tablespoons butter	1 cup chopped mushrooms
2 tablespoons flour	⅓ cup sliced ripe olives
1 cup chicken stock or broth	2 tablespoons chopped pimiento
1 cup cream	
1 teaspoon salt	1 teaspoon lemon juice
¼ teaspoon paprika	2 egg yolks, well beaten
2 cups diced, cooked chicken	2 tablespoons milk

Make a cream sauce by mixing and heating together until thick the butter, flour, chicken stock, cream, salt and paprika. Put the chicken, mushrooms, olives, pimiento and lemon juice into the sauce and heat 5 minutes.

Beat the egg yolks and milk together and add to the above mixture. Stir and cook over low heat 2 minutes.

Putting Together: Cut hot fondue in 2-inch squares, place on individual plates and cover with Chicken à la King, garnishing with parsley and more paprika.

DAY-AHEAD FONDUE
[Serves 8]

2 loaves French bread	4 eggs, well beaten
½ cup softened butter or margarine	5 cups hot milk
½ cup prepared mustard	½ tablespoon Worcestershire sauce
1½ pounds aged Cheddar cheese in ¼-inch slices	1 teaspoon salt
	⅛ teaspoon cayenne

Paprika

As the name implies, this is prepared the day before it is to be used and "aged" in the fridge.

Slice bread ½-inch thick and spread generously with butter which has been blended with mustard.

Fill 4-quart casserole with alternate layers of bread and cheese.

Blend eggs, milk, Worcestershire, salt and cayenne and pour over bread and cheese; sprinkle top with paprika. Cover and refrigerate overnight.

Two hours before serving time, take casserole from refrigerator and let stand at room temperature ½ hour. Preheat oven to 350°.

Bake, uncovered, for 90 minutes. Serve immediately.

FONDUE BEER PUDDING
[Serves 6 to 8]

10 slices white bread	½ teaspoon dry mustard
4 tablespoons (½ stick) softened butter	½ teaspoon salt
10 slices Cheddar cheese	⅛ teaspoon fresh-crushed black pepper
3 eggs	1½ cups beer

Trim crusts from bread; butter slices generously.

In buttered large casserole or baking dish, layer bread slices and cheese.

Beat eggs with mustard, salt and pepper; blend in beer and pour over bread and cheese layers.

Preheat oven to 350° and bake until set and browned, about 45 minutes.

BLENDER BAKED FONDUE
[Serves 6]

4 eggs, separated
1½ cups (about 3 slices) soft, stale breadcrumbs
½ teaspoon salt
1 cup hot water
1½ cups cubed Muenster or Monterey Jack cheese

Beat egg whites until stiff but not dry. Put aside.

Into blender container, place breadcrumbs, water and salt; cover and whirl 1 minute. Stop and add the 4 egg yolks and blend till smooth. Stop blender again and add cheese, blending until cheese is coarsely grated.

Gently fold blender mixture into egg whites. Pour into buttered 2-quart ovenproof baking dish and bake at 350° until done, about 30 minutes.

ROSY RICE FONDUE
[Serves 4 to 6]

1½ cups grated American cheese
1 cup hot cooked rice
1 cup tomato puree
2 eggs, beaten very lightly
3 tablespoons soft butter
¾ teaspoon salt
½ teaspoon white pepper

Blend all ingredients together. Bake in preheated 325° oven, using buttered baking dish, casserole or mold, until done—about 30 minutes.

CREAMY RICE FONDUE
[Serves 4 to 6]

Proceed as above but instead of tomato puree use 1½ cups White Sauce.

BAKED MOCK FONDUE
[Serves 4]

5 egg yolks, well beaten
2 cups soft, buttered bread-
    crumbs
1½ cups milk

½ pound sharp American
    cheese, grated
¾ teaspoon salt
½ teaspoon dry mustard

5 egg whites, beaten stiff

Place egg yolks, breadcrumbs, milk, cheese, salt and
mustard in bowl and blend well. Add beaten egg whites,
folding in gently.

Transfer to 2-quart baking dish or casserole and let
stand 1 hour.

Place casserole in pan of hot water and bake in preheated 325° oven 1 hour.

Variation: For a different flavor, use wholewheat
breadcrumbs.

FONDUE CHEESE PIE
[Serves 6]

¼ pound (1 stick) butter
  Pinch salt
1 pint milk (2 cups)
1 cup flour

6 eggs
1½ cups Gruyère cheese,
    grated
Egg yolk

Put butter, salt and 1 cup of the milk in heavy saucepan and bring to a boil.

Make smooth paste of the flour and other cup milk.
Pour boiling milk mixture into paste, stirring continually to blend well. Return to pan and keep stirring.
Break eggs into mixture, one at a time, reserving some
yolks for top, stirring in between. Add all but 1 tablespoon of cheese and stir until thick and smooth and
creamy.

Butter a deep pie dish and pour mixture in. Brush
egg yolk over top, sprinkle with remaining tablespoon of
grated cheese and bake in preheated 360° oven 30
minutes.

Can be served either hot or cold.

TOMATO FONDUE RAMEKINS
[Serves 4 without crabmeat, 6 with]

2 tablespoons butter or
    margarine
½ cup all-purpose flour
½ teaspoon salt
½ teaspoon dry mustard
3 cups milk
1 teaspoon Worcestershire
    sauce

2 cups grated Emmentaler or
    Gruyère cheese
1 6-ounce package frozen
    crabmeat, thawed (op-
    tional)
4 or 6 slices white toast
4 or 6 tomato slices
Butter

Salt and pepper

Melt butter in top pan of double boiler. Gradually
stir in flour, salt and dry mustard. Add milk and cook,
stirring occasionally, until thickened and smooth. Stir
in Worcestershire and cheese, stirring until cheese is
melted. Stir in crabmeat and cook until crab is heated.

Cut toast diagonally, to make toast points. Place 2
points in individual heatproof casseroles or ramekins.
Divide fondue over top. Place tomato slices in center;
dot with butter; season. Place under broiler until tomato
is lightly browned.

CHILI-TUNA-CHEESE FONDUE SANDWICHES
[Serves 6]

1 can tuna fish
½ cup minced green chilies
    (canned)
½ cup minced celery
2 tablespoons minced onions
    (optional)
¼ cup mayonnaise
1 teaspoon chili powder
¼ teaspoon salt

12 slices sandwich bread
2 cups grated American,
    Cheddar or Muenster
    cheese
3 eggs, beaten
1 cup milk, scalded
¼ cup cream
¼ teaspoon salt
Dash Tabasco sauce

Make sandwich filling of tuna, chilis, celery, onion,
mayonnaise, chili powder and salt, blending well. Spread
on 6 slices of bread, cover with remaining 6. Cut each
sandwich into quarters.

In buttered square ovenproof baking dish place a layer

of sandwich quarters. Sprinkle a layer of cheese. Repeat until all sandwiches and cheese are used.

Combine egg, milk, cream, salt and Tabasco, blending well; then pour over contents of dish. Bake in 300° oven until set and custardy, about 50 minutes.

You may want to trim the crusts off the bread before making the sandwiches.

CRAB FONDUE SANDWICHES
[Serves 4]

1 cup (or 1 6½-ounce can) cooked crab	8 thin slices bread
1 cup diced celery	¼ pound sliced Cheddar cheese
3 tablespoons mayonnaise	2 eggs
1 tablespoon prepared mustard	1 cup milk
Sprinkle of salt	1 teaspoon Worcestershire sauce
Paprika	

Mix crab and celery; blend in mayonnaise, mustard and salt.

Spread mixture between slices of bread, making 4 sandwiches. Cut them in half.

In greased baking dish, alternate layers of sandwich halves and cheese.

Beat eggs; add milk and Worcestershire. Pour over all in baking dish. Sprinkle with paprika; cover. Bake in preheated 325° oven until done, about 45 minutes.

POACHED CHICKEN FONDUE

Still another kind of fondue is served at the Hostellerie de la Poste in Avallon, Burgundy. This is a poached chicken covered with a cream-curry sauce and served on a bed of steamed rice. It is called "La Fondue de Poulet Papa Bergerand," Bergerand being a celebrated chef who liked his chicken poached.

Since the recipe I've seen is complicated to the point of boredom, here is a very agreeable one which achieves lovely taste without tears.

FONDUE DE POULET A LA CREME
[Serves 4 or 5]

1 2½- to 3-pound tender chicken	2½ ounces warmed cognac, Calvados or brandy
4 tablespoons butter	1½ cups heavy cream
1½ cups minced onion	1 teaspoon curry powder
1 cup chicken stock	1 teaspoon flour
1 teaspoon butter	

Cut chicken into serving portions and brown in iron skillet on all sides in butter. Add onion and chicken stock, cover and simmer gently until tender.

Uncover and pour warmed cognac over, set on fire, shaking pan until flames are gone.

Remove chicken pieces to warm serving platter and keep warm.

To pan juices in skillet add heavy cream and curry powder, blend and simmer until sauce is reduced one-fourth.

Make a paste of the flour and butter and when smooth blend into sauce. Then strain sauce through fine sieve and use to blanket chicken pieces. Serve as soon as possible.

Beef Fondues and Other Meats

Fondue Boeuf Bourguignon (Burgundy Beef) is a misnomer, according to the misnomer experts, since the meat only cooks and nothing melts. But fondue is a word that also means table-top cooking, where each eater plonks a morsel of food into a pot.

But whatever, it's too late to change the name to something like "French-Fried Steak," or "Frizzled Tid-Bits," or "Beef à la Deepfat."

Historical purists claim it isn't even Burgundian, but there's that handy legend about the nonstop picker and his pals of that province who dragged their fondue pot along as they frantically stripped the grapes from the vines at their peak of perfection. And since Burgundy is so adjacent to Switzerland, it didn't take long for the news to travel.

There are as many different recipes for Fondue Bourguignon as there are experts, although they differ only in the little details. Basically, you heat up oil or fat in a metal pot and plunge a cube of steak in it for as long as you want it done (and you'll never again be satisfied by the white-capped guy in restaurants, with the baked brains, who cooks your steak the way *he* likes it).

But like the theological debate over the number of angels who can dance on the head of a pin, the controversy is over the little things and it goes on—a small war in print. To save you the trouble of deciding between the bewildering proponents and opponents, I have analyzed a dozen or more recipes and boiled them down to give you a variety of the variations:

Amount of oil for the pot: 2 inches deep/ never more than half full/ ½ to ¾ full/ 3 cups/ 3 to 4 cups.

Kind of oil to use: 3 cups salad/ 1 cup butter to 2 cups vegetable/ vegetable oil only/ combination of butter or margarine and butter-flavored oil/ no butter/ peanut mixed with clarified butter/ ½ corn and ½ vegetable/ peanut or corn/ peanut alone/ coconut fat and peanut/ sunflower seed/ any vegetable/ 2 cups corn and ½ cup margarine/ cooking or ½ cooking and ½ butter/ ½ pound butter and ⅔ cup olive/ no olive.

From Vreni Carol, a transplanted Swiss now in California, comes a variation in the fat to be used for Fondue Bourguignon: ½ olive oil and ½ clarified butter.

The most exotic fat I know of is grape seed oil from France, which does not smoke. It contains herbs from Provence—thyme, laurel (bay leaf) and rosemary. The brand is Soleillou, the manufacturer is Michel Chassone and the cost of a quart is $2.49 at Macy's.

Temperature of oil: 350°/ 360°/ 375°/ 425°/ highest setting on electric fondue pot/ 400° on electric skillet/ bubbling/ when cubed bread browns in 1 minute/ in 30 to 40 seconds/ when drop of water dances on surface/ if the meat sizzles.

To prevent oil spattering: Add 1 teaspoon salt/ toss piece of bread into hot butter/ dry the meat first.

Reusing oil: To clarify oil for re-use, drop a few thick slices of raw potato into the hot oil after it has been used, cook until potatoes are brown and well done; strain fat through cheesecloth and, when cool, refrigerate.

Kind of beef to use: Boneless sirloin/ filet/ shell/ tenderloin/ rump steak/ top round/ round steak, tenderized/ flank steak/ trimmed of all fat/ at room temperature/ at room temperature 30 minutes/ cut just prior to serving/ taken from refrigerator and dried with paper towels.

Amount of meat: 1½ pounds for 4 or 5 people/ 2 pounds for 4 people/ 5 or 6 ounces per person/ ½ pound per person/ 3 pounds for 6 people.

Size of beef cubes: ¾-inch/ 1-inch.

Time in oil: Rare, 10 to 20 seconds/ 20 seconds/ 30 seconds; medium, 1 minute; well-done, 50 seconds/ 50–60 seconds/ 1½ to 2 minutes.

Seasoning: Light salt and pepper before/ no salt and pepper before.

Number of people per pot: 4/ 4 or 5/ 6.

Have on hand: Salt and pepper/ plenty of paper napkins/ finger bowls/ finger bowls with thin slices of lemon or lime floating/ tablecloth that is washable or disposable/ a fire extinguisher.

To drink (see French Wine List for Fondues): "Fresh beer"/ light white, rosé or red wine/ Sangría/ Burgundy/ red Chianti/ hot tea.

What else to cook: Tender pork (always cook thoroughly)/ ham/ lamb/ veal/ boned breast of chicken/ chicken livers/ turkey meat/ blanched sweetbreads/ lamb and beef kidneys, bite-sized/ bite-sized cuts of frankfurter/ cocktail franks/ cocktail smokies/ Vienna sausages/ chopped lamb balls/ Mexican meat balls/ Swedish meat balls.

Note: Do not cook meat fondues and fish fondues in the same oil. Raw shrimp/ halved scallops/ cubed firm-fleshed fish/ chunks of swordfish steak (briefly).

Accompaniments: Sauces (see Staggering Array of Sauces section and Index)/ bottled sauces/ condiments/ vegetable relishes/ pickles/ pickled mushrooms/ pickled onions/ chutney/ salads/ French and Italian bread in cubes/ French-fried onion rings/ breadsticks/ hard rolls/ potato chips/ cranberry sauce/ chopped salted peanuts.

Reminders:
See that burner is always adjusted to keep oil hot throughout meal.
Keep tray under burner to protect table.

Well, you pays your money and you takes your choice. But if you want one definitive recipe, here we go:

A DEFINITIVE BEEF FONDUE
[Serves 4]

½ potful of a cooking oil, preferably peanut (practically smokeless)

2 pounds not-too-expensive steak (rump) in ¾-inch cubes for well-doners, 1-inch for rarers

See that meat is dry and at room temperature. Do not season before cooking. The hep hostess or host will cut the squares of beef to fit the taste of each guest, i.e.: for those who like their meat well-done, thinner cubes and for the very rare palate, thick, square cubes . . . so that all the guests will take the same amount of time to cook their tidbits. Heat oil to just below boiling. Toss in 1 teaspoon salt. Immerse first cubes of beef experimentally until you get the knack of achieving the desired doneness. Salt and pepper afterward, if you want to, but with a decent choice of sauces it seems unnecessary.

Drink whatever you like that is at hand.

Fondue Bourguignon, which hopped across the border from France to Switzerland, or maybe it was vice versa, also leapt across the border from France to Spain, where it is served at the Soley Restaurant in Barcelona as "El Gran Frou Frou."

Despite the name change it is not different from the classic Burgundy Fondue, although the meat is fried in a mixture of peanut oil and clarified butter.

One of the Spanish sauces served is

GARLIC SAUCE
[Makes 1¼ cups]

4 large cloves garlic, peeled
2 egg yolks
1 cup olive oil
1 teaspoon lemon juice
¼ teaspoon fresh-crushed pepper
¾ teaspoon salt

Mash the garlic with the egg yolks, blending well. Add the olive oil, drop by drop, while beating until sauce is consistency of mayonnaise. Stir in remaining ingredients.

A more sophisticated type of Fondue Bourguignon can be achieved by marinating the meat in advance, either several hours ahead or overnight. The ingredients are combined and mixed well in saucepan, brought to a boil and poured over the meat. Then covered and chilled. When ready to use, remove meat and pat dry before cooking.

FAR EAST MARINADE

¾ cup water
3 tablespoons honey
2 tablespoons soy sauce
2 tablespoons salad oil
1 tablespoon vinegar
1½ teaspoons celery seed
1 teaspoon garlic salt
½ teaspoon dry mustard
¼ teaspoon fresh-ground pepper
½ teaspoon powdered ginger

FLEMISH MARINADE

¾ cup beer
1 onion, sliced
1 teaspoon parsley flakes
½ teaspoon salt
¼ teaspoon fresh-crushed pepper
½ bay leaf
1 whole clove
¼ teaspoon crushed rosemary

WINE MARINADE

1 cup red wine
½ onion, diced
1 tablespoon salad oil
1 clove garlic, crushed
¼ teaspoon salt
⅛ teaspoon fresh-crushed pepper
⅛ teaspoon thyme
2 parsley sprigs
1 bay leaf

ORIENTAL MARINADE FOR CHICKEN

1 6-ounce can pineapple-orange concentrate, un-diluted, thawed
¼ cup (½ stick) butter, melted
1 teaspoon soy sauce
1 teaspoon ground ginger

Prepare the same way as beef marinades. Use with any fowl, in same manner.

On the Street of the Four Winds up near the Odéon in
Paris, M. A. Cochet conducts the restaurant Au Savoyard and features two classical fondues—the Cheese
Fondue of Savoie and the Bourguignon au Savoyard.
Knowledgeable Parisians gravitate to this colorful spot,
frequently making a meal of nothing but the two fondues. You will find the cheese recipe (Fondue "Au
Savoyard") in that section. Here is the instruction for
the Beef or Bourguignon pot.

FONDUE BOURGUIGNON AU SAVOYARD

Cubes or strips of rump steak   Peanut oil
Sauces (see below)

Rather than filet mignon, rump steak is the choice
of M. Cochet, because it has more flavor. "You can also
use *contrefilet* or *entrecôte*," he says.

Heat the oil to boiling in fondue pot over kitchen
stove, then bring it to the table with Sterno or alcohol
heat under to keep it hot. Using *wooden* forks or skewers, each diner cooks his meat to the turn he likes in the
hot oil, then dips it into one or more of the sauces.

If practical, each one should have his own plate with
a selection of sauces, some bottled and the rest mixed in
advance.

ELECTRIC MEAT FONDUES

ELECTRIC BEEF FONDUE

Serve 1/3 to 1/2 pound beef tenderloin per person.

Add 3 cups cooking oil to electric fondue pot and heat
at highest setting about 15 minutes, or until a cube of
bread turns brown in 40–60 seconds.

Have various sauces at table, preferably in servings
on a fondue plate with sauce compartments.

CASTLE SAUCE
[Makes 1⅓ cups]

1 cup sour cream
3 egg yolks
1 tablespoon lemon juice
¼ teaspoon salt
½ teaspoon dry mustard
½ teaspoon Worcestershire
   sauce

Place all ingredients in blender container; cover and
process at low until well blended.
Pour into a small saucepan and cook over low heat,
stirring constantly, until slightly thickened. Do not allow
to come to boil. Serve warm.

CAPER MAYONNAISE
[Makes about 1½ cups]

1 cup mayonnaise
⅓ cup capers, drained
¼ teaspoon Tabasco sauce
⅓ cup lemon juice
½ teaspoon onion salt

Place all ingredients in blender container, cover and
whirl at low until capers are minced. Refrigerate until
ready to serve.

CURRY MAYONNAISE
[Makes 1½ cups]

1 cup mayonnaise
3 tablespoons milk
4½ teaspoons curry powder
½ teaspoon Tabasco sauce

Place all ingredients in blender container; cover and
turn on low until they are well blended. Refrigerate
until ready to use.

ANCHOVY BUTTER
[Makes about 1 cup]

1 cup soft butter
2 tablespoons warm milk
2 anchovy filets or 1 teaspoon
anchovy paste
4 sprigs parsley

Place all ingredients in container of blender; cover and whirl at high until well blended. Scrape down with rubber spatula (with power off) to keep ingredients flowing to center. Refrigerate until 30 minutes before serving.

HORSERADISH SAUCE
[Makes about 2 cups]

½ cup heavy cream
½ cup light cream
½ cup prepared horseradish
1 slice dry bread, broken up
1 teaspoon sugar
¼ teaspoon salt
Dash white pepper

Place heavy cream in blender container, cover and whip at low speed until thickened. Turn on and off and use rubber spatula to push cream from sides into center. When whipped, remove to small bowl.

Put remaining ingredients into container, cover and whirl at high speed until well blended.

Remove and add to whipped cream, folding together. Chill in refrigerator until ready for use.

ELECTRIC MEAT FONDUE VARIATIONS

Chicken Breasts: Cut into cubes, pat dry and cook as for beef.

Marinated Chicken: Combine ⅓ cup soy sauce, ¼ cup dry sherry, ¼ teaspoon ground ginger. Put cubed chicken into marinade, cover and chill 1 hour. Just before serving, drain well and dry with paper towels. Cook as beef.

Calf's Liver: Cube and cook as beef.

Fish: Cut 1 pound boned slice (½ to ¾ inches thick) salmon, halibut, or swordfish into ¼ × 2-inch strips. Dip into hot oil until cooked and lightly browned. Then dip into Curry, Tartar or Seafood sauce.

Shrimp: Use 1 pound shelled, deveined, washed and dried raw shrimp. Cook in hot oil until shrimp turns pink. Use same sauces as for fish. For faster cooking, use pre-cooked shrimp.

For an elegant, variety-filled dinner, arrange several of these prepared foods on a platter and surround them with a variety of appropriate sauces. Can be prepared in advance.

Instructions on the napkins at The Wine and Cheese, Chelsea, London:

"FONDUE BOURGUIGNON

"Pick up a piece of raw meat with your fork and dip it into the hot oil. Fry it to your taste and remove it to your plate. Then [using another, cold fork] dip your fried meat into the various sauces. . . . Here we go, we bet you and your friends will like it."

In Rome's vast Piazza Navona one of the two fine restaurants is Tre Scalini (The Three Steps) which is not only famous for its Chocolate Truffle Ice Cream, but for the mixed Roman grill called

FRITTO MISTO ALLA TRE SCALINI
[Serves 4 to 6]

1 pound thin slices veal	Salt and fresh-crushed
1 pound chicken livers	pepper
4 veal kidneys	Oregano
1 small cauliflower	Cooking oil
8 artichoke bottoms	Lemon wedges
1 Italian (small) eggplant	Watercress
2 medium zucchini	Frying Batter (see below)

Pound veal even thinner and cut into medallions 2 inches in diameter. Cut livers in half. Trim core, fat, and sinews from kidneys and cut into cubes.

Break cauliflower into flowerets, slice eggplant and quarter zucchini lengthwise. Blanch the vegetables. Sprinkle meats and vegetables with salt, pepper and oregano.

Heat oil in metal fondue pot to 380° on kitchen stove. Make Frying Batter.

Arrange meats and vegetables on tray or individual plates and bring to table, along with Frying Batter and bubbling fondue pot, which is placed over Sterno. Each diner is given wooden fork or skewer and served with lemon wedges and watercress. He dips a piece of meat or vegetable in batter, then fries it in fondue pot until it is golden brown. This goes on until plates are empty or eaters are full.

Frying Batter

2 cups flour	4 eggs, beaten
1 teaspoon salt	1⅓ cups milk
⅛ teaspoon cayenne	3 tablespoons melted butter

Sift flour, salt and cayenne together.

Blend eggs and milk, then blend mixture with flour, mixing thoroughly. Add butter and mix well.

OTHER MEAT FONDUES

VEAL FONDUE BOURGUIGNON
[Serves 4]

2 pounds trimmed veal filet or shoulder, in cubes	Cooking oil
	2 tablespoons butter
Slice raw potato	

Meat should be dry to prevent sizzling.

Fill metal fondue pot with about 2 inches of oil. Add butter. Place over heat, either in kitchen or at table and bring to a boil, adding potato to prevent fat from spattering. If done in kitchen, transfer to table with heat under to continue bubbling of oil.

Guests spear veal on fork which is dropped into oil so meat can be cooked to desired doneness. Remove, transfer to cold fork and dip in sauces.

Serve with salad and crusty French or homemade-type bread.

Erich Lessing, the *Life* photographer, lives in Vienna, but when I wrote asking for a Viennese twist on a fondue recipe, he was away in Israel. However, his wife, Traudi wrote me: "The only interesting version of a meat fondue we try from time to time is not to use beef only, but to have another serving dish full of rather thinly sliced venison—but you must have the heart to use saddle, as shoulder stays too tough during the short frying period in a fondue pot."

VIENNESE VENISON FONDUE

"If you use the tender parts and your venison is good, this is particularly delightful with all kinds of sweet sauces. You can add a Cumberland Sauce and others of that kind to your usual array of sauces that accompany meat fondues."

DUKE OF CUMBERLAND SAUCE
[Makes about 2 cups]

1 cup sherry   1 glass currant jelly
1 teaspoon Worcestershire sauce

Combine and mix well. Serve cold.

THE INTERNATIONAL FONDUE COOK BOOK   113

HAM FONDUE
[Makes about 2 cups]

2 4½-ounce cans deviled ham   ½ cup sour cream
½ cup condensed cream of   2 tablespoons sherry
    mushroom soup   French bread in cubes

Combine ham and soup in top of double boiler and
heat to boiling over direct heat, stirring occassionally.
Then place over boiling water. Stir in sour cream and
sherry. Cover and heat until warm.

Transfer to preheated fondue dish over flame.

Serve with bread cubes and forks.

An inexpensive fondue is Delmarvalous, named after
the Delmarva Peninsula (Delaware-Maryland-Virginia)
where over a billion pounds of chicken of the broiler-
fryer type are produced every year.

DELMARVALOUS CHICKEN FONDUE
[Serves 3 to 4]

6 cups chicken broth   ½-inch cubes
3 whole chicken breasts,   Salt and pepper to taste
    skinned, boned, cut into   Sauces (see below)

Bring chicken broth to boil in fondue pot and keep it
at that temperature.

Divide chicken among guests and provide each with
either a wooden fork or two metal ones (since metal gets
too hot to put in mouth).

Each guest cooks his own cubes, one at a time, in the
boiling broth for ½ to 1 minute, then dips cooked meat
in one or more of the sauces below.

When the chicken is gone, guests are provided with
cups from which to sip the enriched broth.

CHILEMON SAUCE
[Makes 1 cup]

Grated yellow rind of 1
lemon

1⅓ tablespoon (4 teaspoons)
lemon juice

¾ cup chili sauce

Combine and chill several hours before serving.

CREAMY MUSTARD SAUCE
[Makes 1 cup]

1 tablespoon butter
1 tablespoon flour
½ cup milk

Salt and white pepper [1]
1 tablespoon spicy prepared
mustard

½ cup heavy cream

In saucepan melt butter and blend flour in thoroughly.
Gradually add milk, stirring constantly to produce a
smooth sauce. Season to taste with salt and pepper.

Remove from heat and stir mustard into sauce.

While sauce cools completely, whip cream until it is
stiff. Then fold in the whipped cream and serve.

RAW MUSHROOM SAUCE
[Makes slightly under 1 cup]

½ cup fresh mushrooms, very
finely chopped
⅓ cup sour cream
½ teaspoon lemon juice

¼ teaspoon anchovy paste
¼ teaspoon paprika
Salt and white pepper to
taste

Using cheesecloth or towel, squeeze the mushroom bits
dry. Combine with sour cream, lemon juice and anchovy
paste. Season with paprika and salt and pepper.

---

[1] Why *white* pepper? So that no black specks appear throughout
the sauce.

SIZZLING SAUSAGE FONDUE
[Serves 4]

2½ pounds beef frankfurters, and/or cocktail sausages, Vienna sausages, pork sausages and/or smoked sausages
Peanut oil filling pot ⅔ full

Cut all sausages into bite-sized pieces. Be sure all surfaces are dry.

Heat oil in metal fondue pot to 375° or 400° but not smoking.

Have guests either use wooden fondue forks or skewers, or if metal forks are used, *make sure cooked sausages are transferred to another fork before approaching the mouth.* Or else be sure to invite a doctor.

Dunk in any beef sauce or use some of the ones below.

CONEY ISLAND SAUCE
[Makes ⅔ cup]

½ cup mayonnaise-type salad dressing
3 tablespoons prepared mustard
3 tablespoons pickle relish (or chopped sweet pickles)
½ teaspoon sugar
Sprinkle of salt

Combine ingredients and mix well. Can be served warm, if heated slowly over low flame, but usually chilled and served cold.

CHILI WILLIE SAUCE
[Makes 1½ cups]

1 cup chili sauce (or catsup)
¼ cup brown sugar (packed firmly)
¼ cup water
2 tablespoons Worcesterchire sauce
2 tablespoons prepared mustard
2 teaspoons chili powder
4 drops Tabasco sauce

Combine all ingredients in saucepan, blend well and cook over low heat, stirring occasionally until hot. Can be served immediately or chilled in refrigerator.

Also, for sauces use bottled condiments, such as Mild Mustard, Spicy Mustard, French or English mustards, A.1. Sauce, Sauce Escoffier, Diable Sauce, straight Worcestershire sauce, catsup (tomato, anchovy, walnut) and straight from the bottle chili sauce.

FONDUE VENEZIA
[Serves 4]

1½ pounds calf's liver
2 large Bermuda onions
2 cups olive oil (or 1 cup
   and 1 cup salad oil)
Salt and fresh-ground
   pepper

Remove all pipes and filament from liver; cut into cubes less than 1-inch square.

Slice onions in 1-inch wide rings, then cut crossways, making half-circles.

On skewer or fork, guest fixes first a half-ring of onion, then a cube of liver and immerses in metal fondue pot in which oil is just below bubbling. He cooks the liver and onion to desired doneness, removes and seasons only with salt and pepper, transferring to plate, then uses cold silver fork for eating.

A Staggering Array of Sauces

Here follows a vast assortment of sauces, dressings, dips and suchlike for the flavoring of beef and other meat fondues.

From this collection, choose anywhere from 3 to 8 at one time. You can offer them to your guests, each sauce in a dish or bowl of its own, or on individual compartmented fondue plates (or any large dishes) with a small amount of each sauce—like an artist putting dabs of color on his palette—for each person.

APRICOT-CHUTNEY SAUCE
[Makes 1½ cups]

1 cup apricot preserves   2 tablespoons cider vinegar
½ cup chutney, fine-chopped   1 teaspoon grated lemon peel

Combine all in saucepan; cook over low heat, stirring constantly, until mixture bubbles. May be served hot or cold.

Variation: Use pineapple, peach, plum or berry preserves for a different dip-sauce.

AURORE SAUCE NO. 2
[Makes 1 cup]

1 cup mayonnaise   2 tablespoons catsup
2 tablespoons cognac or   ½ teaspoon Worcestershire
    brandy   sauce
½ teaspoon lemon juice

Combine in order named and blend. Keep chilled until ready to serve.

COLD BARBECUE SAUCE
[Makes about 2 cups]

½ cup chili sauce
½ cup catsup
½ cup dry red wine
¼ cup salad oil
1 tablespoon lemon juice
1 tablespoon olive oil
1 tablespoon Worcestershire
    sauce
½ tablespoon chili powder
1 small clove garlic, peeled

½ medium onion
½ tablespoon barbecue spices,
    or ½ teaspoon each, ore-
    gano, paprika and basil
½ teaspoon fresh-ground
    pepper
½ bay leaf
½ teaspoon kosher or smoked
    salt
1 teaspoon celery salt

Using pint or larger jar with tight lid, mix all ingredients; shake well and store until ready to use. Then
remove onion, bay leaf and garlic and shake well again.
May also be used as marinade for beef, fowl or seafood.

COOKED BBQ CHILI SAUCE
[Makes 2 cups]

3 tablespoons butter
½ cup fine-chopped sweet
    red, green or yellow
    peppers
¼ cup fine-chopped onion
1 or 2 cloves garlic, fine-
    chopped
2 cups canned tomatoes

3 ounces red wine
3 ounces bouillon, or ½
    bouillon cube dissolved
    in 3 ounces hot water
¾ tablespoon chili powder
¾ tablespoon salt
¾ tablespoon cornstarch
¾ teaspoon sugar

⅛ teaspoon pepper

Melt butter, cook pepper, onion and garlic until soft.
Add remaining ingredients and bring to a boil; reduce
heat and simmer until thickened, stirring constantly.
Cover; simmer very gently 10 minutes longer.

TEXAS BARBECUE SAUCE
[Makes 1½ pints]

2 cups water
½ teaspoon fresh-ground
   pepper
1 cup vinegar
1 5-ounce bottle Worcestershire sauce
4 tablespoons butter
4 tablespoons brown sugar
2 teaspoons salt
1 teaspoon garlic salt

Add pepper to water and simmer 5 minutes. Add vinegar, half of Worcestershire, butter, sugar, salt and garlic salt and simmer 5 minutes. Add remainder of Worcestershire sauce and blend well.

BEARNAISE SAUCE
[Makes 1¼ cups]

4 egg yolks
2 tablespoons water
1 tablespoon tarragon vinegar
4 tablespoons cream
1 teaspoon salt
Dash cayenne pepper
8 tablespoons butter
1 teaspoon chopped fresh
   tarragon
1 teaspoon chopped parsley
1 teaspoon chopped chives

Mix egg yolks, water, vinegar, cream, salt and pepper in earthenware or pottery bowl until well blended.

Heat hot water to boiling in saucepan, lower flame and place bowl over saucepan and stir mixture with wire whisk until it begins to thicken. Add butter, a spoonful at a time until total is blended in, then add seasonings and beat until blended and thick.

Serve hot.

Note: If only a small amount is needed, cut recipe in half.

This is from Doris, the wife and daughter-in-law of two Doctor Gospes in the San Francisco Bay area.

BLENDER BEARNAISE
[Makes 1¼ pints]

6 green onions, minced
2 cups butter
4 egg yolks
¼ cup wine vinegar

2 teaspoons dried tarragon
¼ teaspoon dry mustard
¼ teaspoon salt
Dash Tabasco sauce

Sauté onions until transparent in small amount of the butter. Place onion in container of electric blender. Melt remainder of butter over low heat.

Add to blender container the egg yolks, vinegar, tarragon, mustard, salt and Tabasco. Turn blender to medium and mix 2 minutes, then gradually add melted butter until all has been absorbed.

If mixture is too thick, thin with hot water, a teaspoon at a time.

BOB'S BEEF FONDUE SAUCE
[Makes 1¼ cups]

⅛ pound butter (½ stick)
4 tablespoons catsup
4 tablespoons chili sauce
4 tablespoons Worcestershire

sauce
4 tablespoons A.1. sauce
2 teaspoons dry mustard
Salt and pepper to taste

In skillet soften butter over low heat. Add catsup, chili sauce, Worcestershire, A.1., mustard and season with salt and pepper to taste. Blend well and heat thoroughly.

BORDELAISE SAUCE
[Makes 1 cup]

1 tablespoon butter
1 cup fresh mushrooms, chopped (or 1 3-ounce can mushrooms and stems)
1 cup beef bouillon or stock

1½ tablespoons cornstarch
1 tablespoon red wine
1 tablespoon lemon juice
1 teaspoon powdered tarragon
White pepper to taste

Melt butter in saucepan and sauté fresh mushrooms until tender. (Combine canned with melted butter.)

Mix cornstarch well with part of bouillon, then combine with remainder and add to mushrooms in pan. Cook, stirring until mixture comes to boil. Add wine, lemon, tarragon, season with dash of pepper and simmer about 10 minutes.

DEVILED CATSUP
[Makes 2 cups]

2 tablespoons butter
½ cup chopped onion
2 tablespoons flour
2 bouillon cubes dissolved in
    2 cups boiling water
3 tablespoons catsup
½ teaspoon salt

1 tablespoon fine-chopped
    parsley
1 teaspoon bottled mustard
1 teaspoon sugar
⅛ teaspoon fresh-ground
    pepper

Cook onion in butter in pan. When light brown, stir in flour, blending well.

Add dissolved bouillon cubes, stir. Add remaining ingredients and cook, stirring, until mixture thickens slightly. Strain.

CHABLIS SAUCE
[Makes 1 cup]

1 cup Chablis
⅓ cup catsup
1½ tablespoons cornstarch

3 tablespoons water
1½ tablespoons butter or
    margarine

Stir wine into catsup in small saucepan and bring to a boil. Reduce heat and simmer, uncovered, 5 minutes.

Blend cornstarch and water together into paste and stir into simmering wine. Cook, stirring, until thickened and bubbly. Add butter, blend and cook 1 minute more.

CHICKEN/LAMB HOT BARBECUE SAUCE
[Makes 1 pint]

1¼ cups chili sauce
1 cup fine-chopped onion
6 tablespoons olive oil
1½ tablespoons water
1½ tablespoons lemon juice
1 tablespoon tarragon
    vinegar

1½ teaspoons brown sugar
1 teaspoon Tabasco sauce
½ teaspoon salt
½ teaspoon dry mustard
½ teaspoon crushed chili
    pepper
1 clove garlic, fine-chopped

½ bay leaf, crushed

Mix all ingredients in saucepan; bring to boil, reduce
heat and simmer 15 minutes. Serve hot or cold.

LEMON CHILI
[Makes 1 cup]

¾ cup chili sauce
1½ tablespoons lemon juice

Grated rind 1
    medium-to-large lemon

Blend ingredients well and chill before serving.

CHUTNEY SAUCE
[Makes over 1 cup]

1 8-ounce can tomato sauce
    with onions
4 tablespoons chutney,
    chopped

1 teaspoon Worcestershire
    sauce
½ teaspoon salt

Mix and heat the four ingredients together. For ham,
beef or pork fondue.

Now comes a sauce for ham or pork contributed by Major Robert Gardner, USAF (Ret.), which he picked up while attending a sauce course at the Cordon Bleu.

DUKE OF CUMBERLAND SAUCE NO. 2
[Makes 1½ cups]

Fine-grated peel of 2 oranges

1½ cups red currant jelly

2 tablespoons dry mustard

Cover grated peel with water in saucepan. Bring to boil, boil 2 minutes and drain.

Mix mustard with a little water to make a paste. Add grated peel and mix. Add jelly and blend well.

DIABLE SAUCE
[Makes over 1 cup]

2 tablespoons butter
1 small onion, minced
1 clove garlic, minced
1 teaspoon salt
1 teaspoon paprika
1 teaspoon dry mustard
½ teaspoon Tabasco sauce

⅛ teaspoon fresh-ground pepper
Sprinkle cayenne
1 6-ounce can tomato paste
½ cup tarragon vinegar
1 teaspoon Worcestershire sauce

¼ cup bouillon

Sauté garlic and onion in melted butter in saucepan until they are tender.

Combine salt, paprika, mustard, Tabasco, pepper and cayenne and add to garlic and onion.

Blend tomato paste with vinegar, Worcestershire and bouillon and add to saucepan. Cook over low heat 30 minutes, stirring occasionally, until sauce is thick.

Strain through fine sieve. Serve cold.

May be made in double or triple quantities and bottled. Keep in refrigerator.

DILL SAUCE
[Makes 1 cup]

2 dill pickles, minced
⅔ cup sour cream
¾ teaspoon whole or ground
   dill seed, or 1 sprig fresh

dill or 1 teaspoon dried
   dill, crushed
½ teaspoon salt
Pinch fresh-ground pepper

Mix all ingredients together well and chill until ready to serve.

FLAMENCO SAUCE
[Makes over 1 cup]

4 scallions, minced
1 clove garlic, minced

½ cup dry red wine
1 10¾-ounce can beef gravy

Simmer onions and garlic in wine until liquid is reduced to half. Stir in gravy and simmer 5 minutes.

OLD-FASHIONED FRENCH DRESSING
[Makes 3 cups]

½ cup water [1]
½ cup red wine vinegar
1½ tablespoons lemon juice
1 tablespoon salt
1 teaspoon Worcestershire
   sauce
1 teaspoon ground black
   pepper

½ teaspoon sugar
½ teaspoon English dry
   mustard
1 small clove garlic,
   chopped
1½ cups salad oil
½ cup olive oil

Blend together all ingredients except oils. Then add salad and olive oils and mix well again. Chill. Shake before serving.

Keeps well in refrigerator. Can be made and stored in a 1-quart Mason jar.

---

[1] Amount of water used depends on how oily you want dressing.

HARTFORD SAUCE
[Makes ¾ cup]

¼ cup A.1. steak sauce   ¼ pound butter or margarine

Combine A.1. sauce and butter in saucepan. Cook over medium heat until butter is melted and mixture is well blended.

HAWAIIAN DIP
[Makes 2 cups]

1 8½-ounce can crushed   2 tablespoons vinegar
   pineapple, juice and all   1 tablespoon soy sauce
1 8-ounce can tomato sauce   1 teaspoon prepared mustard
            Sprinkle onion salt

Mix all ingredients in saucepan; simmer 20 minutes, stirring once in a while. Serve hot with any meat fondue, except beef.

HELL SAUCE
[Makes 1½ cups]

1 8-ounce can tomato sauce   hot peppers, chopped
4 ounces sharp Cheddar   1 tablespoon prepared
   cheese, shredded (1 cup)   mustard
1 or 2 tablespoons sweet or   3 drops Tabasco sauce

Heat tomato sauce well; add cheese and stir until melted; add peppers, mustard and Tabasco, stir until blended. Serve with meat or frankfurter fondue.

This is vouched for by the National Dairy Council which says it never fails.

RELIABLE HOLLANDAISE SAUCE
[Makes 1 cup]

¼ pound (1 stick) butter
2 egg yolks
½ teaspoon salt

Dash cayenne pepper
1½ to 2 tablespoons lemon juice

Melt butter.

Beat egg yolks until thick; add salt, cayenne and 3 tablespoons melted butter; beat until well-mixed and stiff. Continue beating, adding lemon juice and remainder of melted butter, a few drops of each alternately, until all has been incorporated.

Make enough only for one fondue party, to be used at once. Don't save.

HONG KONG SAUCE
[Makes 1½ cups]

1 8-ounce can tomato sauce
    with mushrooms
¼ cup orange marmalade
¼ cup soy sauce

2 tablespoons lemon juice
¼ teaspoon ground ginger
    (or 1 tablespoon minced
    crystallized)

Dash garlic powder

Mix all ingredients well in saucepan; simmer 5 or 6 minutes. Serve hot with meat or seafood fondue.

MILD HORSERADISH SAUCE
[Makes 1½ cups]

½ cup chili sauce
½ cup mayonnaise
1 tablespoon Worcestershire
    sauce

5 tablespoons prepared
    horseradish
2 teaspoons A.1. sauce

Mix all ingredients together and chill.

RED-HOT HORSERADISH SAUCE
[Makes 2 cups]

1 8-ounce can tomato sauce	3 tablespoons prepared
1 cup sour cream	horseradish (or to taste)

Salt and fresh-ground pepper

Fold tomato sauce into sour cream carefully; add horseradish; season to taste.

Can be served cold or warm with beef fondue. Be careful not to boil.

MINT SAUCE NO. 2
[Makes about 1 cup]

3 ounces mint leaves	1 tablespoon sugar
3 tablespoons wine vinegar	4 ounces water

Wash mint and chop fine. Place in saucepan with vinegar and sugar and simmer gently for 10 minutes. Add water and let cool. Strain out leaves or leave as is.

SWEET MUSTARD SAUCE
[Makes 1½ cups]

5 tablespoons dry mustard	sugar
10 tablespoons confectioners'	Cider vinegar

Mix enough vinegar with the mustard and sugar to make a smooth paste and stir until sugar is completely dissolved.

CURRIED NUTS
[Makes 1 cup]

½ cup grated or flaked coconut	walnuts, pecans, cashews or peanuts, chopped
½ cup salted almonds,	1 teaspoon curry powder

Place all in paper bag and shake well. Spoon out onto sauce plates.

DEVILED MUSTARD SAUCE
[Makes 1 cup]

½ cup dry mustard
½ cup boiling water
½ teaspoon Tabasco sauce

1 tablespoon cooking oil
1 teaspoon salt

Dissolve mustard in water, stirring well. Add remaining ingredients and mix until blended. Let stand at room temperature at least a quarter of an hour.

ORIENTAL MUSTARD SAUCE
[Makes over ½ cup]

3 tablespoons dry mustard   6 tablespoons (3 ounces) Sake

Combine and blend well.

HOTTEST MUSTARD SAUCE
[Makes ¾ cup]

½ cup boiling water
½ cup dry mustard
2 tablespoons salad oil

1 teaspoon salt
Few blades saffron or
    pinch turmeric

Dissolve mustard in boiling water, stirring and blending well. Add oil, salt and for deeper yellow color, saffron or turmeric. Blend again.

PEANUT SAUCE
[Makes ¾ cup]

4 tablespoons heavy cream
2 tablespoons smooth peanut
    butter

2 tablespoons soy sauce
1 tablespoon lemon juice
4 drops Tabasco sauce

Mix together all ingredients and heat gently.

QUICK MEAT FONDUE SAUCES

FAKE BEARNAISE
[Makes ½ cup]

½ cup mayonnaise

1 scallion, fine-chopped

1½ teaspoons tarragon
vinegar

⅛ teaspoon dry mustard

Blend well.

GENEVA SAUCE
[Makes ¾ cup]

½ cup mayonnaise

¼ cup grated Swiss cheese

½ teaspoon dry mustard

Blend well.

RED DEVIL SAUCE
[Makes ¾ cup]

½ cup mayonnaise

¼ cup spicy catsup

½ teaspoon Worcestershire
sauce

¼ teaspoon soy sauce

¼ teaspoon Tabasco sauce

¼ teaspoon chili powder

Blend well.

This sauce for Fondue Bourguignon comes from my cousin, Anne Smith.

REMOULADE SAUCE
[Makes 2 cups]

3 hard-cooked eggs, chopped
    fine
1 egg yolk, raw
1 tablespoon tarragon
    vinegar
3 tablespoons olive oil

½ clove garlic, chopped small
    (optional)
½ teaspoon prepared mustard
Juice of ½ lemon
Salt and cayenne to taste
1 teaspoon horseradish

Mix in order given until well blended.

RUSSIAN DRESSING
[Makes 2 cups]

1 cup mayonnaise
1 sour cucumber pickle,
    chopped fine
3 tablespoons chili sauce
3 tablespoons fine-chopped
    green pepper

2 tablespoons fine-chopped
    sweet red pepper or
    pimiento
½ teaspoon grated onion
2 drops Tabasco sauce

Combine and mix well. Serve at room temperature or
chilled.

SPICY HOT SAUCE
[Makes 1¼ cups]

1 cup chili sauce
½ cup fine-chopped onion
3 tablespoons lemon juice
2 tablespoons salad oil

1 teaspoon brown sugar
1 clove garlic, crushed
½ teaspoon hot pepper sauce
¼ teaspoon dry mustard

Combine all ingredients in saucepan. Heat to boiling;
simmer 5 to 10 minutes. Serve hot.

SOY SAUCE
[Makes 1½ cups]

3 tablespoons butter
1 cup hot water

3 tablespoons soy sauce
1 tablespoon cornstarch

Melt butter in pan; add water and heat to a boil.
Mix soy sauce and cornstarch until a paste results; add
to butter and cook until clear and thickened. Serve warm.

SOY SAUCE WITH GINGER
[Makes 1 cup]

1 cup soy sauce

1 tablespoon ground ginger

In small saucepan blend soy and ginger and bring to
boil.
May be served hot or cold.

SOY-SAKE SAUCE
[Makes 1¼ cups]

¾ cup water

¼ cup soy sauce
¼ cup Sake

Combine and blend well.

CREAMY STEAK SAUCE
[Makes 1½ cups]

1 cup sour cream
½ cup chili sauce

1 teaspoon prepared
mustard
½ teaspoon seasoned salt

Blend all ingredients in small bowl. Chill at least 1
hour. Serve cold.

THICK STEAK SAUCE
[Makes 1½ cups]

½ cup minced green pepper
1½ tablespoons butter or
    margarine
1 8-ounce can tomato sauce
with mushrooms
1 package brown gravy mix
2 tablespoons dry white
    wine or dry vermouth

Sauté pepper in butter 5 minutes. Add tomato sauce and gravy mix, cook until hot and thick, stirring constantly. Add wine and blend.

Serve hot with beef, lamb, ham or pork fondues.

TOMATO STEAK SAUCE
[Makes 1½ cups]

1 8-ounce can tomato sauce
⅓ cup bottled steak sauce
2 tablespoons brown sugar
2 tablespoons cooking oil
½ teaspoon salt

Combine all ingredients in saucepan. Heat to boiling. Serve hot.

ANOTHER STEAK SAUCE
[Makes over 1 pint]

1 cup catsup
1 cup chili sauce
1 tablespoon fine-chopped
    onion
1 tablespoon fine-chopped
green pepper
1 tablespoon fine-chopped
    celery
1 tablespoon Worcestershire
    sauce
1 tablespoon A.1. sauce

Mix ingredients together, adding them in order given. Pour into jar and chill in refrigerator. Shake before serving.

SWEET 'N' SOUR SAUCE
[Makes almost 2 cups]

½ cup minced green pepper   ½ cup water
½ cup minced onion   1 8-ounce can tomato sauce
2 tablespoons butter or   2 tablespoons orange
   margarine   marmalade
1 tablespoon cornstarch   2 tablespoons vinegar
              ½ teaspoon powdered ginger

Cook green pepper and onion in butter over medium heat until tender.

Blend cornstarch with water. Add to vegetables along with remaining ingredients. Simmer 8 or 10 minutes.

Serve hot with lamb, ham, pork or chicken fondues.

SWEET 'N' SOUR SAUCE NO. 2
[Makes 1½ cups]

1 12-ounce jar apricot, peach   1 2-ounce jar pimientos,
   or pineapple preserves   drained and minced
                ¼ cup white vinegar

Blend preserves, pimientos and vinegar well and keep chilled until ready to serve.

TABASCO BUTTER
[Makes ¼ pound]

¼ pound (1 stick) butter   6 drops Tabasco sauce

Butter should be soft. Work Tabasco in well throughout soft butter.

Reshape into stick and chill again. When ready to use, cut into pats or cubes and rub cooked beef, other meat or fish with butter.

SAUCE TARTARE
[Makes 1½ pints]

1 cup mayonnaise
½ cup fine chopped gherkins
  or mild dill pickles
¼ cup capers, chopped fine
2 hard-cooked eggs, sieved
1 tablespoon chopped chives

1 teaspoon chopped tarragon
1 teaspoon chopped chervil
2 chopped green olives
Pinch dry mustard
Dash cayenne pepper
Wine vinegar

In medium mixing bowl, blend all ingredients except vinegar; then add that slowly until right degree of tartness is achieved, blending well.

THOUSAND ISLAND DRESSING
[Makes 1 cup]

½ cup mayonnaise
3 tablespoons catsup or chili
  sauce
3 tablespoons whipped
  cream

1 small hard-cooked egg,
  chopped fine
1 tablespoon chopped sweet
  or sour pickles
½ pimiento, chopped

Blend all ingredients thoroughly.

SAUCY TOMATO SAUCE
[Makes about 1½ cups]

1 8-ounce can tomato sauce
1 carrot, grated
2 tablespoons butter or
  margarine, melted
2 tablespoons water

2 teaspoons sugar
2 teaspoons white vinegar
1 teaspoon Worcestershire
  sauce
1 teaspoon A.1. sauce

¼ teaspoon Tabasco sauce

Blend all ingredients in saucepan. Place over medium heat and simmer 5 minutes, stirring. Serve hot with meat or seafood fondues.

TOMATO RELISH SAUCE
[Makes 1¼ cups]

1 cup chili sauce   ¼ cup pickle relish
                    ¼ teaspoon Tabasco sauce

Stir and blend ingredients together.

Rosemary Cartwright, Rome-oriented in fondue-making, advises: "For Beef Fondue use only olive oil and add clarified butter to keep from smoking" and adds her favorite dip:

SALSA VERDE
[Makes about 1 cup]

3 cloves garlic   3 tablespoons parsley, chives
3 tablespoons basil   or watercress, or 1
3 tablespoons Romano   tablespoon each
   cheese   1 tablespoon fresh-chopped
   Salt and pepper   capers
½ cup olive oil   3 tablespoons wine vinegar

Grind in a mortar the garlic, basil, Romano cheese, diced, and salt and pepper to taste. Add oil slowly until absorbed. Mix and add greens and capers, grinding all into paste. Add vinegar and blend.

YANKEE CATSUP
[Makes about 2 cups]

1⅓ cups strained tomatoes   2 teaspoons dry mustard
   6 ounces vinegar   ¼ teaspoon ground cloves
2⅔ tablespoons brown sugar   Dash fresh-ground black
   1 tablespoon salt   pepper
                ⅛ teaspoon ground ginger

Combine and simmer all ingredients until quantity is reduced to half. Serve hot or cold.

EPICURE YOGURT SAUCE
[Makes 1 cup]

1 cup plain yogurt
1½ tablespoons minced shal-
    lots
½ teaspoon salt
½ teaspoon celery seed
1 grind, fresh-ground pep-
    per

Combine all ingredients well and refrigerate before using.

Variation: Substitute minced green onions and other seeds for shallots and celery seed.

Mixed Bag of
Miscellaneous Fondues

One of the notable Roman dishes, especially featured in the age-old Jewish quarter restaurants near the Tiber, is Carciofi alla Giudia. This makes a unique vegetable fondue, but you must seek out the smallest, most tender young artichokes and do half of the cooking beforehand.

ARTICHOKES ROMAN-JEWISH STYLE
[Serves 4]

12 little artichokes	½ teaspoon fresh-ground
Juice of 1 lemon	pepper
1 teaspoon salt	3½ cups olive oil

Remove tough outer leaves and snip off thorny tips of the little artichokes. Spread leaves open and remove hairy, spiny "choke." In other words, leave only edible leaves and trim stem of woody part. Soak artichokes in water to cover mixed with the lemon juice. Drain dry and sprinkle inside leaves with salt and pepper.

Heat olive oil in deep frying pot or metal fondue pot until bubbling and fry artichokes, 3 or 4 at a time, for 8 to 10 minutes over medium flame. Remove to paper towels and reserve oil. Chill artichokes 2 hours or more.

Reheat oil at serving time to 385° and bring to table in fondue pot. Arrange half-cooked artichokes on platter or serve 3 to each guest on individual plates. Guests pierce stem end of artichoke with fondue fork and place in oil. Artichoke leaves will open, flower-like, curling and turning dark golden. They will become as crisp as potato chips. Remove to plate and eat leaves and bottom hot, with a bit of salt.

If you like mushrooms in your fondue, here's your dish.

FONDUE ALLA FUNGHI
[Serves 4]

1 pound Fontina cheese, diced	fine-chopped
2 tablespoons flour	1 tablespoon butter
1 cut clove garlic (optional)	2 cups dry sherry or Marsala
½ cup fresh mushrooms, fine-chopped	1 tablespoon lemon juice
	2 tablespoons kirsch
1 tablespoon green pepper,	Fresh-ground pepper and nutmeg to taste

Dredge cheese cubes in bowl with the flour, mixing well.

Rub pottery fondue pot with garlic clove.

Sauté mushrooms and green pepper in butter in a skillet for 4 minutes.

Place wine in pot or casserole over moderate heat and cook until small bubbles rise to top. Do not boil. Add lemon juice, mushrooms and green pepper. Toss in cheese ¼ at a time, stirring continually until melted before adding more; keep stirring until fondue starts to bubble a bit. Add kirsch, pepper and nutmeg and blend well by stirring.

Place on table over heat which will keep fondue just below boiling point.

Fry ¾-inch squares of bread in butter and use for spearing and dunking.

EGG FONDUE
[Serves 4]

1 pint olive oil or 1 pound butter, clarified	8 eggs
	Salt and fresh-ground pepper

Heat oil in metal fondue pot until smoking. Break and drop eggs in one at a time and deep fry, browning on both sides. Remove with slotted spoon, drain on paper towels and repeat until all eggs are cooked. Meanwhile, keep fried eggs hot until served.

Serve with crisp bacon, sautéed mushrooms or fried tomatoes.

HAM AND EGG CUTLETS
[Serves 2]

3 tablespoons butter	½ cup smoked ham
3 tablespoons flour	Oil
1 cup milk	Breadcrumbs
4 eggs, hard-cooked	Beaten egg

Make sauce by melting butter in pan, adding flour and blending, then adding milk and cooking slowly to thicken.

Chop eggs fine and put through sieve.

Cut ham into small pieces, add to eggs and sauce. Let cool.

Shape into small cutlets and place in refrigerator. (This can be done ahead of time.)

Heat oil in fondue pot to 350°.

Dip cutlets in beaten egg and breadcrumbs and drop into pot for about 2 minutes per side.

FONDUE WITH BACON
[Serves 4]

4 slices bacon	pepper
1 8-ounce can tomato sauce with onions	⅛ teaspoon garlic salt
⅛ teaspoon fresh-crushed	½ cup shredded Cheddar cheese

Fry bacon, drain and crumble. In saucepan, mix with tomato sauce, garlic salt and pepper; simmer 5 minutes. Add cheese, stir well until melted and lumpless.

Transfer to fondue pot or chafing dish. Keep warm and use as dip for toasted squares of French bread.

Almost any Cheese Fondue, leftover or prepared especially, can thicken with cooking, then be chilled, breaded, and fried as croquettes in deep fat as a sort of double fondue.

DOUBLE FONDUE
[Serves 4]

2 cups cheese fondue, thickened	1½ tablespoons olive oil
Melted butter	2 eggs
1 cup sifted all-purpose flour	Salt and pepper to taste
	2 cups stale fine white breadcrumbs

Oil for deep frying

Spread fondue on a large buttered platter in a layer 1-inch thick. Brush melted butter all over top. Chill in refrigerator until firm.

Meanwhile spread flour in a plate.

Beat eggs with the oil and season to taste, in a soup plate.

Spread breadcrumbs in a large plate.

Cut chilled fondue into 1-inch cubes. Roll each in the flour, dip into egg on all sides thoroughly, drain off excess egg, roll in breadcrumbs, patting them in place all over with flat side of knife. Roll cubes again in beaten egg, then in crumbs, being sure to cover well so they will not explode in frying. Let stand 1 hour.

In fondue pot (metal) heat cooking oil to 385° and bring to table where it will cook over Sterno. Bring cubes of breaded fondue on individual plates, and let guests carefully cook their own to a golden brown. Drain on paper towels.

PARMESAN FRITTERS
[Serves 6]

1 cup cooked white meat chicken, diced	cheese
	Salt and pepper
6 ounces lean cooked ham, diced	3 egg yolks
	Oil for deep-fat frying
1⅓ cups grated Parmesan	Fritter Batter (see below)

2 cups Tomato Sauce

Ahead of Time: Combine chicken and ham in mixing bowl; add cheese, season; fold in egg yolks and mix well. Form walnut-sized balls with palms of hands.

At Table: Heat oil in fondue pot until almost smoking.

Dip balls in Fritter Batter, fry in oil until crisp and golden on outside. Heap on round platter that has been covered with napkin. Serve with Tomato Sauce on the side.

FRITTER BATTER
[Makes about 1 cup]

3 eggs	¼ teaspoon salt
2 tablespoons sifted flour	Pinch cayenne pepper

⅓ cup cream

In bowl, beat eggs with flour; add seasonings; add cream gradually. Batter should be smooth and syrupy.

ANCHOVY FRITTERS

Use flat filets of anchovy; soak in cold water to remove salt.

Drain; dry between two towels. Cover filets with the above Fritter Batter and, one by one, plunge them in very hot oil; cook until golden.

Drain well. Cover serving platter with napkin and place filets in a pyramid. Decorate with sprigs of fried parsley and lemon halves.

RICOTTA PILLOWS
[Serves 4 to 6]

2¼ cups flour
2¼ tablespoons butter
½ teaspoon salt
1¼ pounds Ricotta cheese
2 eggs

3 tablespoons grated Parmesan cheese
Peanut oil for deep-fat frying
Spaghetti sauce

Ahead of Time: Work flour with butter and salt, gradually adding enough lukewarm water to make a dough that is soft but does not stick to the hands in the kneading. Shape dough into a smooth ball, cover. Let stand for 1 hour.

Roll out dough on lightly-floured board until thin. Cut with a cookie cutter into circles about 2½-inch in diameter.

Mix Ricotta, eggs and Parmesan in bowl.

Place 1 generous teaspoon of this filling on each round of dough, fold over into half-moons and pinch edges together firmly, so none of the filling will escape.

At Table: Heat oil to 370° in fondue pot and let each eater fry his own, until they (the pillows, natch) are golden brown. Serve with any spaghetti sauce.

Here is a filling for tarts, turnovers, croquettes or crêpes which also goes by the name of fondue in France.

FONDUE FILLING
[Makes 2 cups]

2½ tablespoons butter
3 tablespoons flour
1½ cups boiling light cream or milk
½ teaspoon salt
Pinch white pepper

Pinch cayenne pepper
Pinch nutmeg
1 egg yolk
1 cup Emmentaler cheese, cubed
2 tablespoons butter

Cook 2½ tablespoons butter and flour together over low heat in large saucepan without browning. Remove and beat in boiling cream; add salt, pepper, cayenne and nutmeg. Return to heat, bring to a boil, stir for 1 minute and remove from heat again. Taste for seasoning.

Drop egg yolk into sauce and beat in briskly with wire whip, continue to beat air in for 1 minute to cool, then whip in cheese and 2 tablespoons butter. If not used immediately, cover with film of butter to keep from forming a skin.

Dessert Fondues

Hot-in-the-pot participation desserts are becoming increasingly popular, for they are a most felicitous way to wind up a dinner of togetherness.

Among the new Fondue Desserts I've cooked up are these first six happy endings. The first caters to a secret desire almost everyone has.

DUNKIN' DOUGHNUT DIP
[Serves 4]

8 doughnuts, plain or sugared	Sugar
4 cups strong hot black coffee	Cinnamon
Cream	Chocolate syrup

Serve each person with 2 doughnuts and a cup of coffee. Have cream, sugar, powdered cinnamon and chocolate syrup on side.

Let each add seasonings desired to coffee, but do not drink.

Dunk doughnuts in coffee, either whole and held in fingers, or in 1-inch bites speared on forks, depending on gentility of gathering.

Addition of chocolate syrup turns coffee into mocha. Fun!

Now that we've got our feet wet, try this one:

STRAWBERRY SHORTCAKE FONDUE
[Serves 4]

½ pint (1 cup) whipping
    cream
½ cup confectioners' sugar

1 teaspoon lemon juice
½ plain chiffon cake
1 quart fresh strawberries

Mix cream and sugar in saucepan, bring to boil, stirring constantly; let boil 30 seconds, remove to fondue pot and keep over very low heat to prevent scorching. Add lemon juice.

Cut cake into 1-inch cubes and toast lightly.

Hull and clean strawberries. Blanch 30 seconds in boiling water.

Spear first a cube of cake, then a strawberry on wooden fork, dunk in cream and cover well, remove and eat.

Plain angel food cake may be substituted for chiffon.

FRUITS IN LEMON-ORANGE SAUCE
[Serves 4]

Sauce

Juice of 6 lemons
                Juice of 6 medium oranges
Sugar to taste

Strain juices, combine with enough sugar to suit your taste and simmer 10 minutes. Transfer to fondue pot over simmering heat.

Fruits

Sections of tangerines or
    oranges
Chunks of pineapple or pear
Slices of peaches, nectarines
    or apricots
Melon balls sprinkled with
    lemon juice

Stoned cherries
Seedless grapes
Seeded dates
Canned mandarin sections,
    drained
Drained cocktail fruits

Pierce each piece of fruit with a wooden skewer or a long toothpick; put in single layer on waxed paper in freezer tray. Chill in freezer 2 hours.

Remove and defrost slightly for 10 minutes.

Method: Dip fruit into warm sauce until coated. Remove and eat.

Four, or at most, six people are maximum to crowd around one fondue pot.

BANANA SPLIT FONDUE
[Serves 4]

Hot Chocolate Sauce

9 squares sweet chocolate,	up
or 3 3-inch bars, broken	½ cup heavy cream

Melt chocolate in cream in top of double boiler, stirring constantly. Transfer to fondue pot over low flame.

Strawberry preserves	Vanilla ice cream, soft
Pineapple preserves	One banana for each person,
Whipped cream	in 1-inch thick rounds,
Chopped nuts	sprinkled with lemon juice

Method: On a large serving platter or palette, place strawberry and pineapple preserves, whipped cream, nuts and in center, the ice cream.

Serve each person with a sliced banana and fondue fork and spoon. Dip slices first into Hot Chocolate Sauce, then hold over pot until dripping stops. Now spoon preserves, ice cream, whipped cream and nuts over chocolate banana slice on individual plate.

HOT SCOTCH KISSES
[Serves 4]

Carmel-Butterscotch Sauce

½ cup light corn syrup	4 tablespoons butter
1 cup brown sugar (packed)	⅔ cup medium cream
	½ teaspoon vanilla

In saucepan, cook syrup, sugar, butter and cream together over low heat until mixture becomes thick and creamy, let cool slightly and add vanilla. Transfer to fondue pot and keep warm over very low heat.

Method: Brush sugar and starch from 20 marshmallows, serve 5 to each person along with wooden fork. Dip marshmallows in caramel-butterscotch sauce to cover completely, drip off excess sauce over pot, twirling fork, or let cool on plate. When all marshmallows are dipped and eaten, divide remaining sauce among diners.

Variation: Instead of marshmallows, serve unsalted popcorn and do likewise.

Variation No. 2: Instead of Caramel-Butterscotch Sauce, use Hot Chocolate Sauce from Banana Split Fondue.

PIPPINS AND CHEESE
[Serves 4]

3 tablespoons butter	1½ tablespoons kirsch or
3 tablespoons flour	brandy
1 cup milk	4 or 5 pippin apples, cored,
2 cups diced sharp Cheddar	peeled and cut in
cheese	¾-inch chunks

Melt butter in fondue pot; slowly add the flour, mixing well. Stir in milk slowly until fondue becomes thick. Add cheese a little at a time, stirring each time until melted, then add kirsch and blend.

With wooden forks, dip apple chunks and cover with sauce. Apples should be crisp—either new or chilled.

In New York City now, "For Two Cents Plain" (a glass of carbonated water) has gone up to ten cents. In like manner, the nickel candy bar, which had retailed at a dime, is now 15¢. Which probably makes this recipe a bit expensive, since most 15¢ candy bars weigh 1½ ounces and you need 6 of them.

CANDYSTORE FONDUE
[Serves 4 or 5]

6 1½-ounce candy bars   to Peanut Butter Cups)
   (anything from Mounds   ½ cup medium to heavy cream

Break up bars, combine with cream in fondue pot or
blazer pan of chafing dish and stir over low heat until
melted and smooth.

Variations and Additions: Use 9 ounces of straight
milk chocolate, bittersweet or orange-flavored chocolate.

Add ½ cup chopped pistachios, almonds, peanuts, wal-
nuts or pecans.

Spice the fondue up with ½ teaspoon of ground all-
spice, anise, cardamom, cinnamon, coriander, ginger,
mace, mint, nutmeg or cloves.

Add 1 tablespoon of freezer-dried coffee.

Or add 2 tablespoons of liqueur, such as curaçao,
kirsch, plum, cherry or apple brandy. Or 2 tablespoons
of sherry, Madeira, Marsala, Port or Concord grape wine.

Dippers: Toasted or stale sponge cake, fingers of chiffon cake, broken sections of angel food cake, fingers of
gingerbread, ladyfingers, slices or chunks of pear, apple,
peach, plum, apricot, nectarine; sections of orange,
mandarin orange or tangerine.

FESTIVE FONDUE
[Serves about 8]

2½ cups confectioners' sugar   3 tablespoons favorite
  ½ cup (1 stick) butter, soft   liqueur (curaçao,
  ½ cup boiling water   Grand Marnier, kirsch,
  ½ cup Chablis, Sauterne or   etc.)
    other light white wine

Cream sugar and butter together, working in boiling
water until smooth; add wine and liqueur and blend.

Place in fondue pot over medium heat at table.

Dips: Any mentioned in Candystore Fondue (above),
plus strawberries, marshmallows, coffee cake, croissants,
brioche cubes or Brazil nuts.

FONDUE TRIFLE

1 recipe Festive Fondue
(above) in pot, hot
Toasted or stale chiffon,
pound, sponge or angel
food cake squares or strips
Macaroons
Custard sauce
Whipped cream

Thawed box of strawberries
in syrup (or any other
berries)
Marmalade (orange,
pineapple, ginger)
Chopped nuts
Chopped mixed candied
fruits

Each guest is given an individual bowl. He dips pieces
of cake or cookie into the fondue pot, swirls it to coat
well, then places in bottom of bowl.

Then, from larger serving bowls, he adds whipped
cream, custard sauce, berries and nuts to taste; then more
soaked cake, repeating the process until he has as many
layers as desired.

ROYAL MOCHA FONDUE
[Serves 4]

½ pound bittersweet
chocolate
½ cup strong coffee

3 tablespoons cream
3 tablespoons cognac or
brandy

¼ teaspoon powdered cinnamon

Melt chocolate in coffee in fondue pot over medium
heat, stirring with wooden fork or spoon until smooth.
Add cream, cognac and cinnamon, continuing to stir
until mixed thoroughly.

Dippers: Marshmallows, cubes of angel food cake,
slices of fresh peaches, candied orange peel, etc.

Tip: If sauce becomes too thick, add more coffee,
liqueur or cream, according to taste of company.

MONK'S INN CHOCOLATE FONDUE
[Serves 4]

Use hard Norwegian or other hard chocolate bar, mixed
with ¼ the amount of Swiss milk chocolate, a little

water and cherry brandy or kirsch. Finish in fondue pot or top of double boiler over boiling water. Cook 10 minutes. If too liquid, add a little heavy cream.

Serve hot, immediately, and keep hot.

Another lovely recipe from my cousin, Anne Smith of Pittsburgh.

TOBLERONE FONDUE
[Serves 6]

4 3-ounce bars Toblerone milk chocolate, or other with honey and nut chips

½ pint cream
1½ ounces (3 tablespoons) Kaluah or crème de cocoa (optional)

Break chocolate into pieces in top of double boiler over hot, but not boiling, water; add cream and stir until melted.

Put in fondue pot over medium flame; add liqueur. Do not let chocolate boil.

Dippers: Squares of pound, sponge or chiffon cake; fingers of angel food cake or ladyfingers; pitted dates and prunes; strawberries, cherries and seedless grapes; chunks of apple, pear and nectarine.

Variations: Toblerone has introduced a new bar, containing almonds and honey but with bittersweet chocolate. Substitute these for all or part of the milk chocolate bars.

By coincidence, Mrs. Siegfried Mohr of San Jose sent me a similar recipe, but she recommended 1 ounce (2 tablespoons) of brandy, Cointreau, peppermint liqueur or 1 tablespoon of powdered instant coffee.

And among the dippers: Marshmallows, pineapple chunks, dried apricots and banana chunks.

CHOCOLATE PEANUT FONDUE
[Makes over 2 cups]

1 can sweetened condensed milk	¼ cup peanut butter
	⅛ teaspoon salt
2 1-ounce squares unsweetened chocolate	½ to 1 cup hot water
	½ teaspoon vanilla

In top of double boiler put milk and chocolate. Cook over hot water, stirring, until chocolate melts. Add peanut butter and salt and cook until thickened. Remove from heat and slowly stir in hot water until sauce is desired thickness. Stir in vanilla.

Transfer to fondue pot and dip in marshmallows or any desired dunkers.

CREAMY FUDGE FONDUE
[Makes 1⅓ cups]

3 squares unsweetened chocolate	¾ cup sugar
	2 tablespoons butter
½ cup light cream	Dash salt
¾ teaspoon vanilla	

Place chocolate and cream in saucepan; stir constantly over low heat until chocolate is melted and mixture is smooth and blended. Add sugar, butter, and salt; continue cooking, stirring constantly, 3 to 5 minutes longer, or until slightly thickened.

Remove from heat and add vanilla.

Pour into a small fondue pot or chafing dish to keep warm.

Fresh or dried fruits, candies, cookies, ladyfingers and snack foods are served along with the fondue.

CHOCOLATE-COVERED FRUIT FONDUE
[Makes 2 cups, serves 4]

2 6-ounce packages
    semi-sweet chocolate
    morsels
½ cup sugar
1 teaspoon vanilla
2 tablespoons dark rum
    (very optional)

½ cup light cream
3 to 4 cups fruit in bite-size
    pieces (banana, apple,
    orange, seedless grapes,
    cherries, strawberries,
    etc.)

Place all ingredients except fruit in fondue saucepan.
Place directly over flame (Sterno or alcohol) and stir
until chocolate is melted and mixture is smooth. Partially
cover or lower flame so mixture is kept just warm.

Spear pieces of fruit with fondue forks, wood skewers
or long picks and dip into fondue. Swirl to remove excess chocolate.

My lovely little niece, Joyce Levinson, seems to have great
success with this dessert.

JOYCE'S FRUIT A LA FONDUE
[Serves 4]

1½ pounds of peeled and
    trimmed fruit, in cubes
    or squares (such as fresh
    peaches, pears,
    cantaloupe, apples,
    nectarines, plums,

honeydew or Cranshaw
    melon)
Batter for Fruit (see
    below)
Peanut oil
Confectioners' sugar

Prepare fruit cubes.

Make Batter for Fruit. Bring both to table. Fill metal
fondue pot ⅔ or ¾ full of peanut oil, bring to bubbling
point, either on stove or at table.

When guests assemble, they spear either from serving
platter or individual plates, a square of fruit on fondue
fork, dip it into batter, let excess drip back, then plunge
fruit into oil until browned. Fruit is removed from fork,

sprinkled with confectioners' sugar and the delicious morsel is eaten with a cold fork.

BATTER FOR FRUIT

⅓ cup sifted flour	2 eggs, beaten
2 tablespoons sugar	⅔ cup milk
2 tablespoons baking powder	1 tablespoon salad oil or
½ teaspoon salt	melted shortening

Sift dry ingredients together.

Blend eggs, milk and oil. Add dry ingredients and mix until a smooth batter is achieved.

PETER FONDUE
[Serves 4]

1 cup chicken consommé	1½ tablespoons curry powder
1 cup Concord grape or	1 tablespoon arrowroot
Marsala wine	1 tablespoon cold water

Simmer consommé, wine and curry together, blending well. When well mixed and hot, put in fondue pot on table over low heat.

Mix arrowroot with water and add to pot, stirring until thickened and smooth.

For Dipping: Chilled fruits, such as strawberries, chunks and balls of cantaloupe, Cranshaw, casaba, or any other melon (except, perhaps, watermelon), drained seckel pears, sections of tangerine, pineapple chunks and cherries.

Wooden skewers are ideal for use here.

WHAT TO DUNK FOR DESSERT

There is a wide range of tidbits which can be dipped into the many different flavored dessert fondues—fruits, candies, cookies, cake cubes, even nuts.

And a dessert fondue, while a happy ending for any

meal, can also comprise an afternoon or late evening snack.

Also, after dipping, the morsel can be rolled in chopped nuts or flaked or shredded coconut.

The smaller fruits can be left whole and the larger ones cut into convenient bites or balls. To prevent apples, peaches, bananas or pears from darkening sprinkle with ascorbic acid powder—or lemon juice. The fruits and other dunkers can be arranged attractively on trays, individual plates or fruit shells, such as melon or pineapple halves, scooped out.

Allow from 1/2 to 1 cup of fruit, or 6 to 8 pieces of cake for each serving.

Apple chunks
Apricot halves
Bananas in 1-inch rounds
Cherries
Maraschino cherries
Candied cherries and
    other fruits
Coconut cubes
Seeded dates
Fresh, ripe figs
Seedless grapes
Mandarin orange sections
Melon balls
Orange segments
Papaya dice
Peach pieces
Pear squares
Pineapple chunks
Plum halves
Pitted prunes

Strawberries
Tangerine sections

Marshmallows, plain, co-
    conut and chocolate
Gumdrops
Candied ginger
Candied orange and other
    citrus peel

Sponge, chiffon and angel
    food cake squares
Cookies
Nabisco wafers
Gingerbread squares
Pound cake cubes
Ladyfinger halves
Tiny meringue shells
Small cream puff shells
Doughnut rounds

Large salted nuts, such as Brazils, walnut and pecan halves.

FRIED FRUIT PIES
[Makes 6]

Pastry for 2-crust pie (see below)
1½ cups fruit [1]

Sugar to taste
Confectioners' sugar, sifted

Fat for frying

Roll pastry out about ⅛-inch thick; cut into 5-inch circles.

Sweeten fruit to taste; place about 2 tablespoons on each circle, fold pastry over to form half moons and seal edges with fork tines. Prick tops in several places. These can be made ahead of time and refrigerated.

Heat oil or fat in fondue pot to 375°.

Give each guest a pie (at room temperature) and let him fry it in oil until golden brown on both sides, about 3 minutes. Remove to paper towels, drain off excess fat and sprinkle with confectioners sugar.

PASTRY FOR 2-CRUST PIE
[Makes 2 9-inch piecrusts]

2½ cups all-purpose flour
1 teaspoon salt

⅔ cup vegetable shortening
4 to 6 tablespoons ice water

Sift flour and salt together into mixing bowl.

Divide shortening into 2 portions. Cut half into flour until it is extremely fine. Cut second half into the mixture until lumps of shortening are size of a large pea.

Place mixture in refrigerator and chill thoroughly.

Remove and blend in with a fork just enough ice water to hold dough together. Be careful not to have the dough too wet.

Roll out on floured canvas-covered board with covered rolling pin to ⅛-inch thickness.

---

[1] Almost any fruit can be used: berries of any kind, sliced plums, peaches, cherries, nectarines, pears, apples, seedless grapes, all either raw or cooked; cooked dried apples, peaches, apricots, prunes or raisins.

BRIDE'S FINGERS
[Makes about 1½ pounds]

2½ cups sifted flour
1½ cups butter or margarine
1½ cups sugar
⅛ teaspoon salt
1 tablespoon orange juice

Milk
Flour
Vegetable oil for deep fat
  frying
Warmed honey

Blend flour, butter and sugar; add salt, orange juice and enough milk to form a smooth pastry.

Roll into sausages the size and shape of a bride's finger, roll in flour and drop into boiling oil in fondue pot. Drain with slotted spoon onto paper towels. While still warm, dip in warmed honey.

ELECTRIC DESSERT FONDUES

CHOCOLATE FONDUE
[Serves 6 to 8]

2 cups chocolate chips
⅓ cup dry milk

1 teaspoon vanilla (or
  almond) extract
½ cup boiling water

Place all ingredients into blender container, cover and whirl at high speed until smooth and glossy.

Pour into electric fondue pot and warm over medium heat, stirring constantly. Reduce heat for serving.

Dip in cubes of angel, chiffon or sponge cake, marshmallows, assorted chunks of fruit, Brazil nuts and/or walnut halves.

LEMON FONDUE
[Serves 6]

¾ cup hot water
¼ cup butter
½ cup confectioners' sugar
2 tablespoons cornstarch
2 strips lemon rind, 2 by

½-inch
6 tablespoons lemon juice
  or ¼ cup undiluted
  lemonade concentrate
1 tablespoon rum

Place water, butter, sugar, cornstarch and rind into blender container, cover and whirl at high until rind is finely grated.

Pour into electric fondue pot and cook over medium heat, stirring constantly, until thick and shiny. Stir in lemon juice and rum. For serving, reduce heat.

Dippers: Squares of gingerbread and angel food cake, orange sections, pineapple chunks, whole strawberries.

FRUIT FONDUE
[Serves 4 to 6]

1 12-ounce package frozen   1 teaspoon cornstarch
    strawberries, thawed   2 tablespoons orange liqueur

Place everything in blender container, cover and process at high speed until smooth.

Pour into electric fondue pot and cook over medium heat, stirring constantly, until thick and shiny. Reduce heat for serving.

For dipping: Cubes of sponge, chiffon and angel food cake; doughnuts, assorted pieces of fruit.

Variations: Instead of strawberries, use packages of frozen peaches, raspberries or apricots. Or huckleberries, blueberries or boysenberries.

Or use 1 pound strawberries or other *fresh* fruit, sugared, or 1½ cups canned apricots or peaches, with syrup.

CHOCOLATE FONDUE NO. 2
[Serves 6 to 8]

6 squares unsweetened   1½ cups sugar
    chocolate   ½ cup butter
1 cup light cream   ⅛ teaspoon salt
              2 teaspoons vanilla

Heat all ingredients except vanilla in electric fondue pot at high, stirring occasionally until chocolate is melted. Reduce heat to medium and continue cooking,

stirring constantly until thickened, about 5 minutes.
Add vanilla and mix well. Set heat at low for serving.

SWISS FONDUE CHOCOLAT
[Serves 4 to 6]

3 3-ounce bars bittersweet   ½ cup heavy cream
  Swiss or Dutch chocolate   2 tablespoons orange liqueur

Melt chocolate in cream in electric fondue pot at high
heat, stirring occasionally to mix. When well blended,
add liqueur and stir well. For serving, set control at low.

MOCHA CHOCOLATE FONDUE
[Serves 4 to 6]

1 tablespoon butter   1 7-ounce jar marshmallow
2 squares unsweetened   creme
  chocolate   ⅓ cup coffee liqueur

Melt butter, chocolate and marshmallow creme together in electric fondue pot at high, stirring occasionally to mix. When well mixed, add liqueur and stir well.
Set control at low for serving.

BUTTERSCOTCH FONDUE
[Serves 6 to 8]

¼ cup butter   (packed)
2 cups light cream   1½ tablespoons cornstarch
1 cup dark brown sugar   3 tablespoons light rum

Heat butter, cream and sugar in electric fondue pot
at high, stirring until melted and bubbling.
Mix cornstarch and rum together. Pour into cream
mixture, stirring constantly until well blended. Reduce
heat to medium and continue cooking and stirring until
mixture thickens. Set control at low for serving.

HONEY-ORANGE FONDUE
[Serves 6 to 8]

½ cup butter
1 cup heavy cream
¼ cup honey

¼ cup orange marmalade
1½ tablespoons cornstarch
¼ cup orange liqueur

Heat butter, cream, honey and marmalade in electric fondue pot at high, stirring constantly until melted and bubbly. Reduce heat to medium.

Mix cornstarch and liqueur together. Add to cream mixture and continue cooking, stirring constantly, until thickened. For serving, set control at low.

The Panasonic Party Cooker recipe book has a number of difficult, time-consuming dessert recipes. But this is their version of the standard chocolate dip.

CHOCOLATE FONDUE
[Serves 8]

1 12-ounce package
    semi-sweet chocolate
    pieces

¼ cup butter
⅓ cup coffee liqueur or ⅓
    cup strong black coffee

Set control at 240°. Heat butter in electric pot until just melted. Stir in chocolate pieces until melted. Turn control to off. Blend in liqueur or coffee.

Cake in 1-inch cubes, cookies or fruit are skewered and dipped into the fondue.

The Presto Automatic Fondue recipe book, *Fondue Flair*, has some interesting desserts.

CREAM FONDUE
[Serves 4]

1 cup miniature
    marshmallows

2 tablespoons powdered
    sugar

⅔ cup whipping cream

Pour 1 cup water into base of an automatic fondue
pot. Position tray, rack and bowl over. Plug unit into
outlet.

If you have no electric pot, use double boiler.

Combine whipping cream, marshmallows and powdered sugar in bowl; stir until blended.

Dip in peaches, sponge cake, strawberries.

Variations:

Carmel Cream Fondue: Substitute brown sugar for
powdered sugar. Dip in apples and popcorn.

Crème de Menthe Fondue: Add 1 tablespoon Crème
de Menthe. Dunk ladyfingers, mini-meringue shells.

Peppermint Cream Fondue: Add crushed peppermint
candy to taste. Cover banana chunks, miniature cream
puffs.

Nutty Cream Fondue: Add ½ cup chopped nuts or
crushed peanut brittle to any of above cream fondues.

CHOCOLATE-LIQUEUR FONDUE
[Serves 4]

4 ounces (4 squares) baking   ½ cup whipping cream
    chocolate   1¼ cups confectioners' sugar
            2 tablespoons kirsch

Pour 1 cup water into automatic fondue base. Position
tray, rack and bowl over. Plug into outlet.

Place baking chocolate in bowl and melt. Add whipping cream, sugar and kirsch. Stir until creamy.

For dipping: Maraschino cherries, miniature cream
puff shells, orange sections, plain, chocolate or coconut
marshmallows.

CHOCOLATE-LIQUEUR FONDUE
[Serves 4]

½ cup chocolate syrup   2 teaspoons orange or
    1 cup miniature   apricot liqueur or
        marshmallows   brandy

Over hot water combine syrup and marshmallows, stirring frequently until creamy. Add liqueur and blend.

Into this, dip banana chunks, miniature meringue shells, cubes of cake.

SIMPLE FONDUE DUNK
[Makes 1 cup]

½ cup evaporated milk
1 cup miniature

marshmallows
1 tablespoon apricot brandy

Follow procedure for Cream Fondue (p. 159) or heat over hot water in top of double boiler.

Combine evaporated milk, marshmallows and brandy and stir until well blended. Angel food cake and dates make interesting dunkers.

LOW-CALORIE CHOCOLATE FONDUE
[Serves 4 or 5]

½ cup skim milk
2 teaspoons cornstarch
1 egg yolk
1 6-ounce can low-calorie
   chocolate topping

⅓ teaspoon instant coffee
   powder
Low-calorie canned fruits
   for dipping

Combine skim milk, cornstarch and egg yolk. Beat until blended.

Stir in chocolate topping, coffee powder and ⅓ cup juice drained from one of the fruits. Cook and stir over low heat in electric fondue pot until mixture bubbles and thickens.

Skewer and dip in the fruits, coat well, drip and eat.

PEPPERMINT FONDUE
[Serves 3 to 4]

½ pound thin chocolate mints   3 tablespoons cream

Combine mints and cream in electric fondue pot. Stir and melt over low heat until melted. Keep on low heat while serving.

CARAMEL FONDUE
[Serves 4]

⅔ cup light cream   ½ cup miniature
14-ounce package caramels   marshmallows
              1 tablespoon rum (optional)

Put cream and caramels into electric fondue pot, turning heat to low. Stir while caramels melt. Add marshmallows and mix until blended. Add rum and serve. If fondue becomes too thick, add a little more cream.

LIST OF DUNKABLES

Fruit Dips

Cherries   Banana chunks
Strawberries   Peach slices
Mandarin oranges   Tangerine sections
Grapefruit wedges   Grapes
Apple slices   Pineapple chunks

Pastries and Such

Angel food cake   Marshmallows
Pound cake   Doughnuts
Ladyfingers   Cream puff pastry
Macaroons   Popcorn

For the finishing touch, offer small dishes of chopped nuts, coconut, or finely crumbled cereals for coating.

Again, this is a recipe which can be made in any electric or flame-heated fondue pot.

ELECTRIC FRUITS TEMPURA
[Serves 4]

2 apricots	1 pear
1 peach	1 banana

Batter

½ cup all-purpose flour	¼ teaspoon salt
½ cup water	¼ teaspoon baking powder
1 tablespoon sugar	Dash cinnamon
½ tablespoon cornstarch	Salad or peanut oil for deep frying

Halve apricots and peach, remove pits and quarter; pare and quarter pear after coring; peel and quarter bananas lengthwise, then cut across middle.

Make batter: Combine flour, water, sugar, cornstarch, salt, baking powder and cinnamon and beat until well-blended.

Set automatic thermal control of Party Cooker to 360° and add oil to mark (about 4 cups in Panasonic). Heat until pilot light goes off.

Dip fruits, at end of skewers, in batter and coat evenly. Let excess batter drip back into batter bowl.

Place batter-covered fruits into hot oil and cook until golden brown—3 to 5 minutes. Lift out by skewers or with a slotted wooden spoon. Place on draining rack for 3 minutes to drain oil.

Serve with a sweet sauce.

Wine Lists for Fondues

FRENCH

All of these go well with cheese fondues. Those preceded by a B are also harmonious with beef and other meat fondues. Those with a D are dessert wines, too. And an F means the wine goes well with fish.

B F	Anjou	F B	Graves
D	Barsac	B	Hermitage
B	Beaujolais		Jura yellow
B	Bordeaux claret		Macon
B	Bourgueil	B	Médoc
B D	Champagne	F	Meursault
B	Châteauneuf-du-Pape	B	Pomerol
			Pouilly-Fumé
B	Chinon	B F	Riesling
B	Côtes-de-Beaune		St. Émilion
B	Côte-de-Nuits		Sancerre
	Côtes-du-Rhône	D	Sauternes
	Côtes-Roties	B D F	Vouvray
F D	Gewürztraminer		White Arbois

OTHER WINES FOR FONDUES

Amontillado sherry
Bardolino
Bernkastler
Conchay Toro-Pinot Blanc (Chile)
Cream sherry

Dole
Dry White port
Fendant de Sion
Johannisberger
Lambrusco
Leibfraumilch

164

May Wine
Neuchâtel
N.Y. State champagne
Port
Sangría

Soave
Traminer
Valpolicella
White Moselle

Fondue Equipment[1]

BURNER-TYPE: USING STERNO, ALCOHOL OR SPECIAL FUEL

There are two main divisions: earthenware and metal. The first is for cheese and broth, which require flat-bottom pots and non-stick interiors; and the second must be resistant to the higher heat of boiling oil.

ALBISOLA COOPSTOV: (Italian) Small ceramic Fondue Pot, created for Rosenthal (Netherlands) $10. Macy's.

ALCO: (Japanese) Medium-large capacity Fondue Pot, all chromium, color-matched tray, $29, Bloomingdale's.
   Chocolate Pot, small, stainless steel, $7.50.

ALEXANDER'S DEPARTMENT STORES: 2-quart, enamel-aluminum Fondue Pot, Sterno burner and tray, on sale, $3.77.

AUBECO: (Japanese) Blue Dutch enamel, large pot, Macy's.

BFB: (Bavarian) Enamel, $19.95, Gimbel's.

BAZAR: 6 Long Island and New Jersey stores, 2-quart, enamel, colors, wood base, 6 forks, $8.88.
   2-quart, pewter-finish brushed aluminum, iron base, $9.99.
   Carousel Susan Fondue Set with 2-quart enamel pot, colors, revolving 6-section tray.

BLOOMINGDALE'S DEPARTMENT STORES: (Japanese) Solid copper, aluminum interior, $22.50.
   (U.S.) Copper and stainless steel interior, $29.

---

[1] Where prices are given, they are the ones quoted in stores in New York City in the Fall of 1970.

BONGUSTO: (Italian) Copperware with tin lining, $19.99, Gimbel's.

CATHERINEHOLM: (Norwegian) Enamel Fondue Pot, colors, $12.50, Macy's.

CHRISTIAN WAGNER (West German) Fondue Pot, copper and stainless steel, $25, Bloomingdale's.

CIRCA 21 by Volrath: (U.S.) Stainless steel, 2-quart covered saucepan Fondue Dish, $14.95, fits Flambeau Table Service, $19.95; for Beef Fondue, add Chafer Insert (1½-quart casserole and double boiler) $8.95, A. L. Cahn & Son, Inc. Pot Rack.

COPCO: (Danish) Porcelain enamel on cast iron, colors. 2½-quart Fondue Set with 8 forks, $30; 2-quart, colored, cover, warming stand, $22.

COUNTRY CASUAL: (Taiwan) Small dessert pot, decorated, colors, $7.99, Korvettes.

CULINEX: (Swiss) Fondue Sets (see Spring).

DANSK: (Danish-French) Heavy Fondue Pot, color, $29.95, Bloomingdale's.
    Blue Enamel Fondue Pot, $21.95, base $9.95, Macy's.

DOLPHIN: (Japanese) Fondue Sets, Gimbels.

DOURO: (Portuguese) Solid copperware, tin-lined, Fondue Set, 1¾-pint pot, brass stand and fuel container, copper tray, $22, Gimbels.

DURO: (Japanese) Stainless steel, with tray, medium size, $17, Bloomingdale's.

EAST NEW YORK SAVINGS BANK: Fondue Set, heavy gauge aluminum with bonded enamel finish. Free if you open a new savings account of $500 or more.

EPICURE: (German) Enamel Fondue Pots.

ETCO: (U.S.A.) Heavy enamel Fondue Pot; lid, wood base, $35.99, Macy's.

FORTUNOFF STORES: New York and Long Island, Fondue Set, 2-quart colored enamel pot, black hood, walnut base, Sterno burner, 6 color-coded steel forks, $8.88, on sale.
    2-quart stainless steel pot, black wrought iron stand, Sterno burner, $5.99, on sale.

FRENCH: 2-quart coquelin (earthenware casserole with handle), $13.50, on sale, The Pottery Barn.

GIMBELS DEPARTMENT STORES: Small Chocolate Pot, colors, candle heat, $4.99.

Heavy ceramic Fondue Set with tray and 4 sauce dishes, $6.99.

Small ceramic cheese pot and base, $8.99.

Enamel pot and base, $8.99.

(Japanese) Fondue Set, turquoise, $9.99.

Enamel and stainless steel Fondue Set, 6 forks, $12.99.

Fondue set with 4 plates and 4 forks, $12.99.

Beef Fondue Set, copper, large, $22; 2-quart, $16.99. 2-quart stainless steel, $17.99.

Fondue Set, stainless steel, wood base, cover, 4 forks, $19.99.

Fondue Set with tray, 6 glass sauce trays, 8 forks, $29.99.

Fondue Set with metal base, heavy porcelain, 4 forks, $39.95.

HEIMSCHMUCK: (German) Decorated copper Fondue Set, $24.99, Gimbel's.

ITALIAN: pewter, $25.99, Gimbels.

Copper, tin interior Fondue Set, $75, Bloomingdale's.

Spun steel Fondue Set, $19.99, Korvettes.

JAPANESE: 2-quart stainless steel Fondue Pot, $9.99.

Large Beef Fondue Pot, stainless steel, $14.99, Korvettes.

Large copper Fondue Pots, $21.99 and $23.50, Gimbels.

Large stainless steel Fondue Pot, $20, Macy's.

KORVETTES STORES: (Japanese) Ceramic Fondue Pot, decorated, forks and plates, liquid fuel, small, $9.99.

Large, wooden base, 6 glass trays, 8 forks, Sterno.

LA CREUSET: (French) Beef Fondue Set, red, wrought iron burner, adjustable alcohol heat, 4 forks, $29.95, Princeton Gourmet.

LANDERT: (French) Earthenware Fondue Pot, glazed interior, $5.50; glazed inside and out, $8.00; large, decorated, $11.50, Bloomingdale's.

MACY'S DEPARTMENT STORES: hammered copper Fondue Set, $19.99; smooth $16.99 with tray; larger, $19.99 (Currier Shop).

Small ceramic Chocolate Fondue Pot (Japanese), colors, $5.99.

Fondue Pot (Japanese) enameled, colors, with tray, $7.99.

Small all-ceramic Fondue Pot, tray, $10.99.

Larger (Japanese) with tray $11.88.

THE PAMPERED KITCHEN: Greenwich Village, Spring and other quality Fondue Sets.

THE POT RACK, A. L. Cahn & Sons, Inc. Carries full line of Circa 21 by Volrath, and Spring.

PRINCETON (N.J.) GOURMET: Mexican earthenware Fondue Pot, decorated, lid, burner, forks, tray, 4 bibs, $10.95.

Enamel Fondue Pot, lid, stand, warmer, plate, colors, $12.50.

Copper Fondue Set, 1½-quart wood-handle pot and lid, 6 forks, alcohol burner, copper tray (specify beef or cheese).

PRINZ: (German) Enamel Fondue Set, color, elaborate base, $34.95, Macy's.

ROSTFREI: (German) Stainless steel Fondue Set, liquid fuel, $19.95, Gimbels.

ROYAL: (West Germany) glazed enamel and stainless steel Fondue Sets, $19.99, Gimbels.

RUBEL: Fondue Sets, at World of Cheese, Westport, Conn.

SIGG: (Swiss) Medium, copper and stainless steel, wrought iron stand, wood tray, $27.50, Bloomingdale's.

SPANISH GOURMETWARE: (Breck's of Boston) Covered 2-quart Fondue pan, tray and stand, alcohol burner, porcelain on steel, patterned and colors, $14.95.

SPRING: (Swiss) Most comprehensive line of quality Fondue equipment, starting with 6 braziers in wrought iron, copper, stainless steel, black sheet metal, with wood and metal bases and trays; all equipped with wickless Spring safety burners.

2 flameproof Fondue Casseroles of earthenware, green and rustic design, yellow/brown; a Cheese Fondue Set, consisting of brazier, casserole, 6 forks.

18 different Fondue Bourguignon Sets, in red, orange, green, stainless steel, rustic (bronze patina), copper and silver-plate; some finished in Culinox and Silinox, double-layered materials with inside of stainless steel and exterior of copper or silver.

TAGUS: (Portuguese), small copper Fondue Pot, $9.99, Korvettes.

TAIWAN: Metal Fondue Pot with 6 forks and tray, $7.99, Korvettes.

VULCANIA: (Italian) Individual Chocolate Fondue Pots, $5, Macy's.

WIDE WORLD IMPORT BAZAAR: Pasadena, North Hollywood, Beverly Hills, Calif. Wide assortment of popular-priced (Japanese) Fondue Sets, brass Hot Pots, also known as "Steamboats," Ho-Ko Pans, smaller Japanese versions, wok sets, wooden skewers, etc.

ELECTRIC FONDUE POTS

These are fairly recent appliances and most have the advantage of thermostatic controls and Teflon lining.

ELECTRIC FONDUE BY CORNWALL: (U.S.) with lid, colors. $20, Macy's; $19.99, Korvettes.
    Korvettes, aluminum, some models with Teflon lining, 1½-quart capacity, for beef, cheese or chocolate. Other models, 2-quart capacity with different heaters and handles, $24.95; all models with set of 4 forks, temperature controls.

OSTER: (U.S.) Teflon-lined aluminum pot, no-tip heat base; for cheese, meat, dessert; colors, thermostatically heat controlled, 12-foot cord, 6 forks. $30, Bloomingdale's; $29.99, Korvettes and Gimbels.

PANASONIC: (Japanese) Multi-Purpose Party Cooker, with cover, draining rack, automatic thermostat control, Teflon-coated cooking surface; $29.99 at Gimbels.

PRESTO AUTOMATIC FONDUE: (U.S.) Similar to Panasonic, plus 8 forks; $23.99 at Gimbels.

BUTANE FONDUE BURNER

RONSON: uses tubes of butane fuel; comes in adjustable 12-point flame with high to low control and cast iron stand, chrome trim, $32.50; double burner on wrought iron stand, $49.50; cookette with 6-point flame, $13.50; butane refills, $1.49.

FONDUE FUELS, LIQUID

PIERRE MARCHANT FONDUE FUEL: (alcohol) Essex Mfg. Co., Greensboro, N.C. 27401; for alcohol burners; smokeless and odorless; poisonous if taken internally, flammable; 1 pint, $1.50.

STERNO CHAFING DISH LIQUID FUEL: Sterno, Inc., New York 10022; for liquid alcohol burning units; non-toxic, smokeless, lemon-scented; flip top spout, plastic container; flammable, keep away from eyes and children, 12 ounces, $1.35.

FONDUE FUELS, SOLID

STERNO CANNED HEAT COOKING FUEL: in 2½-ounce and 7-ounce cans. The well-known, safe and reliable, established 1887. There's no fuel like an old fuel.

FONDUE PLATES AND FORKS

All of the stores listed above, and all department and hardware stores, carry many varieties of compartmented beef fondue plates in different colors and materials. The same is true for fondue forks, although I caution against metal forks for oil-cooked fondues, since there is danger of burning the mouth and lips, unless the food is transferred to another cool fork. Wooden forks or skewers are recommended.

DEEP FAT THERMOMETER

A deep fat thermometer, available at household utensil and hardware stores, is an extremely valuable piece of equipment.

Index

Index

INDEX

SOUP'S ON!